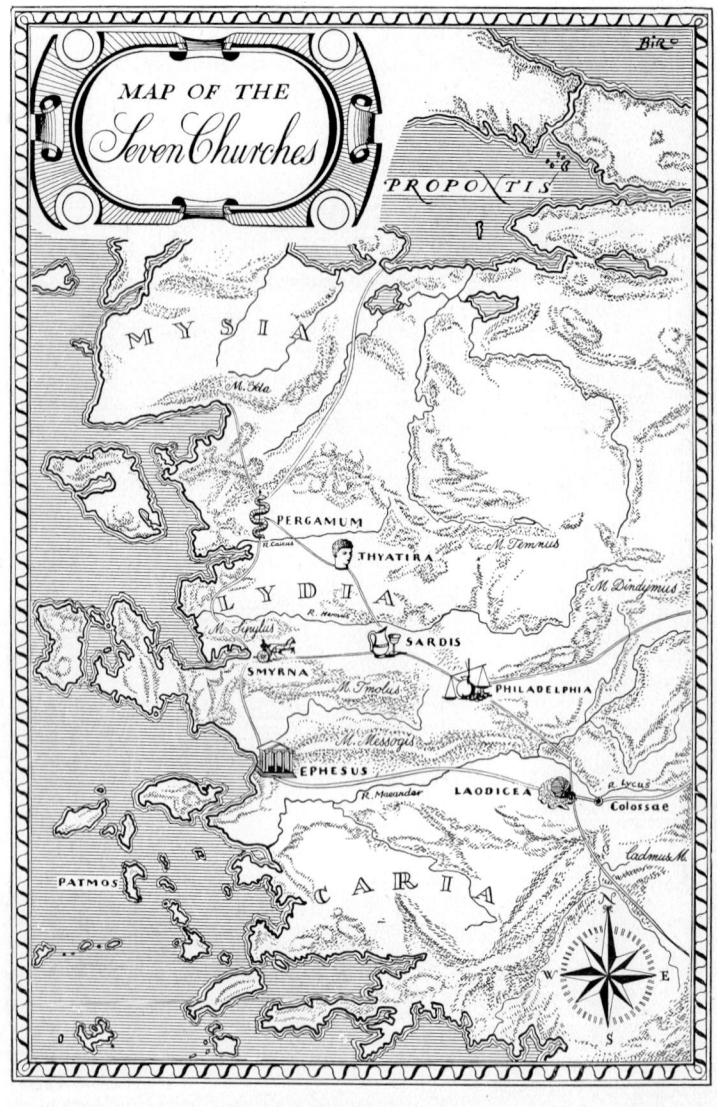

TORCH BIBLE COMMENTARIES

General Editors

THE REV. JOHN MARSH, D.PHIL.
Principal of Mansfield College, Oxford

THE REV. DAVID M. PATON, M.A.
Editor, SCM Press

THE REV. ALAN RICHARDSON, D.D.
Professor of Christian Theology in the University of Nottingham

FOREWORD TO SERIES

The aim of this series of commentaries on books of the Bible is to provide the general reader with the soundest possible assistance in understanding the message of each book considered as a whole and as a part of the Bible.

The findings and views of modern critical scholarship on the text of the Bible have been taken fully into account. Indeed, it is our view that only on a basis of sound scholarship can the message of the Bible be fully understood. But minute points of scholarship, of language or archaeology or text, have not been pushed into the foreground. We have asked the writers of the various books to have in mind the view that the Bible is more than a quarry for the practice of erudition; that it contains the living message of the living God.

The 'general' reader whom we wish to help is therefore not only of one type. We hope that intelligent people of varying interests will find that these commentaries, while not ignoring the surface difficulties, are able to concentrate the mind on the essential Gospel contained in the various books of the Bible. In brief, the TORCH BIBLE COMMENTARIES are for the thoughtful reader who wishes to understand his Bible.

Volumes in the series include:

Already published
  GENESIS I-XI, by Alan Richardson
  DEUTERONOMY, by H. Cunliffe-Jones
  RUTH AND JONAH, by G. A. F. Knight
  ESTHER, SONG OF SONGS, LAMENTATIONS, by G. A. F. Knight
  THE BOOK OF JOB, by Anthony and Miriam Hanson
  II ISAIAH, by C. R. North
  DANIEL, by E. W. Heaton
  ST. MATTHEW, by G. E. P. Cox
  ST. MARK, by A. M. Hunter
  ACTS, by R. R. Williams
  ROMANS, by A. M. Hunter
  II CORINTHIANS, by R. P. C. Hanson
  GALATIANS, by J. A. Allan
  PHILIPPIANS AND COLOSSIANS, by F. C. Synge
  HEBREWS, by W. Neil
  REVELATION, by R. H. Preston and Anthony Hanson

In preparation
  EXODUS, by G. Henton Davies
  I ISAIAH, by C. Witton-Davies
  JEREMIAH, by H. Cunliffe-Jones
  EZEKIEL, by B. Roberts
  AMOS AND MICAH, by John Marsh
  SAMUEL, by D. R. Ap-Thomas
  EPHESIANS, by John Allan
  EZRA-NEHEMIAH-CHRONICLES, by P. R. Ackroyd
  JAMES, by E. C. Blackman
  I AND II THESSALONIANS, by W. Neil
  I AND II PETER, JUDE, by C. E. B. Cranfield
  I AND II KINGS, by Eric Heaton

THE REVELATION OF SAINT JOHN THE DIVINE

Introduction and Commentary

BY

RONALD H. PRESTON
AND
ANTHONY T. HANSON

SCM PRESS
56 BLOOMSBURY STREET LONDON WC1

First published September 1949
Reprinted June 1951
Reprinted March 1955
Reprinted March 1957

Printed in Great Britain by
BILLING & SONS LTD.
GUILDFORD AND LONDON

CONTENTS

INTRODUCTION

		Page
1.	The Purpose of the Commentary	9
2.	Rival Interpretations and Modern Discoveries	12
3.	Characteristics of Apocalyptic Literature	15
4.	The Contents of the Apocalypse	17
5.	Who wrote Revelation?	23
6.	When was Revelation written?	25
7.	Leading Ideas of Revelation	27
8.	Is Revelation a Christian Book?	29
9.	The Old Testament in the Book of Revelation	34
10.	John's Literary Technique	42
11.	The Devotional Use of Revelation	46
12.	Some Useful Books	48

COMMENTARY

I.	Prologue (ch. 1)	53
II.	The Letters to the Seven Churches (ch. 2 and 3)	59
III.	The Vision of Heaven (ch. 4 and 5)	70

	Page
IV. Three Series of Judgments (ch. 6 – 16)	78
(*a*) The Seven Seals (ch. 6)	78
1st Parenthesis (ch. 7)	82
(*b*) The Seven Trumpets (ch. 8 – 9; 11. 14-19; 13)	85
2nd Parenthesis (ch. 10 – 11. 13)	87
3rd Parenthesis (ch. 12)	90
4th Parenthesis (ch. 14)	99
(*c*) The Seven Vials (ch. 15 – 16)	105
V. The Fall of Rome (ch. 17 – 20. 3)	110
VI. The Millennial City (ch. 20. 4-10; 21. 7 – 22. 2, 14, 15)	123
VII. The Last Judgment (ch. 20. 11-15)	127
Note on the re-arrangement of ch. 20 – 22 and the Two Cities	129
VIII. The Eternal City (ch. 21. 1-6; 22. 3-5)	138
IX. Epilogue (ch. 22. 6-13, 16-21)	143
Map of the Seven Churches	*Frontispiece*

INTRODUCTION

1. The Purpose of the Commentary

There is no doubt that the Revelation of St. John the Divine is both the least read and at the same time the most misunderstood of all the books of the New Testament. The ordinary Christian simply does not know what to make of it, so it has been left as the happy hunting-ground of cranks; in the words of E. F. Scott, 'More than any other writing in the Bible, it has attracted the fanatical and curious-minded, and the Church has been too willing to abandon it to them as their natural prey'.[1] Quite recently, two able, convinced and well-instructed Christians were talking about it; one confessed that, apart from hearing a 'star' passage read in church occasionally (principally at funerals), he had not read the book at all because he suspected he would not understand it, and the other said she had come to the conclusion that she never would understand it this side of the grave. Again, a group of keen, adult Christians revealed an amazing sense of relief when, at a parish Bible class which was studying Revelation, the proper setting of the lurid visions in the book was explained; apparently such pictures as 'blood up to the bridles of the horses' had been crudely impressed on them by an ill-informed Sunday School teacher, and the resulting youthful fears and nightmares had never quite left them in adult life.

These experiences are typical of many. Yet the book is in our New Testament and, putting it at its lowest, there is no prospect of its being removed. The only result of neglecting it is to abandon it to 'the fanatical and curious-minded', who not only mislead the ignorant but are liable

[1] *The Book of Revelation*, p. 188.

to bemuse and worry the ordinary Christian unless he understands the book himself. It seems therefore a matter of urgency that Christians should master the book and be at home in it. But there is much more to be said than this. Although the negative reason of being able to combat cranks may start us on the enterprise, yet we shall not have got far before we realise that the essential themes of Revelation are nowhere else in the New Testament so thoroughly and forcefully treated. It was for this reason that the Church finally decided to include the book in her Scriptures, despite its difficulties, and was undoubtedly right to do so. Revelation works on a larger canvas than any other book of the New Testament. Most of the rest of the New Testament is concerned first and foremost with telling the Good News of Jesus Christ. Its writers did not look ahead much; they were hardly concerned with politics or the world of nations. They had their urgent message to deliver. Most of them expected the end to come very soon. So does Revelation, but it paints a large canvas; it deals with nations and with the whole sweep of history seen in the light of God's disclosure of himself in Jesus Christ. In this it has affinities with the Old Testament whose writers often were concerned with nations and with the course of world history. If we did not possess Revelation we would be less clear how this element in the Old Testament is to be understood by those who have seen God supremely revealed in Christ.

The idea of this commentary was conceived as the result of the interest aroused by the authors' study together of the Greek text of Revelation in the evenings of a summer holiday. It is written for the Christian who is not at home in the ancient languages but wants to have an intelligent grasp of the Bible, perhaps because he is a day- or Sunday-school teacher, or lay reader or preacher, or because he realises that regular Bible study is a Christian duty. Perhaps also he reads the Bible Reading Fellowship[1] notes or some other system of passages and notes daily, and would like a plain guide to what appears to be an incomprehensible book. It follows the text of the Authorised Version (A.V.) not because that is the

[1] Details from B.R.F., 171 Victoria Street, S.W.1.

INTRODUCTION

best, but because it is likely to be in the hands of most readers. Where the Revised Version (R.V.) is better on important points, mention will be made of the fact. Thus the present commentary can be used with either version. Generally speaking, the R.V. in the editions with the Apocrypha, the valuable marginal Biblical references and the alternative readings is the best for Bible study. Modern translations like Moffatt, Weymouth, Smith and Goodspeed and the new American Revised Standard Version are also useful. The fact that most readers may have only an A.V. at hand has modified the commentary in other respects. References to Jewish Apocalyptic literature which greatly influenced John (see section 2 of the Introduction below) have been reduced to the minimum necessary to understand Revelation, and even references to the Apocrypha, which unfortunately is missing from too many editions of the Bible, have been included somewhat sparingly. On the other hand, both the Old Testament and the rest of the New Testament are frequently referred to; the Old Testament because echoes of it are found in practically every verse, the New Testament to show that Revelation really is a Christian book, contrary to the opinion of many. Since the Old Testament was undoubtedly the main influence on John's mind (apart, of course, from the fact of Christ himself), and since most of the rest of the New Testament was written in the generation or so before John wrote, we can grasp an enormous amount of the wholeness of the Biblical faith and the fundamental unity of the Bible by a judicious looking up of cross-references. This the commentary will encourage.

Our debt to the various large-scale commentaries on the Greek text is immense, particularly that of the late Archdeacon R. H. Charles in the *International Critical Commentary* series (2 vols.). Comparison with other commentaries reveals clearly the greatness of Charles's work, even though one cannot always agree with him. Here it should be said that there are great differences between commentators on the *details* of the interpretation of the Book of Revelation, and readers who turn to other commentaries after this will find some points very differently treated, e.g.

in Kiddle's commentary in the *Moffatt* series. On the *fundamental principles*, however, we think there is broad agreement. We have tried to avoid speculative theories and all but a few essential re-arrangements of the text, and have endeavoured to concentrate on bringing out the permanent theological meaning behind the categories in which John clothes his thought, and to show how far they are essential to an adequate Christian understanding of God and his purposes as they work out in the history of the world.

2. Rival Interpretations and Modern Discoveries

It would be pleasant to be able to begin the commentary straight away without having to bother about an introduction. But there are so many strange features of the book that it would greatly hold up the commentary to have to deal with them there, and in fact a reading of it is so much helped by an adequate background that there is no alternative but to cover a number of points first. For it is not as though the 'blood up to the horses' bridles' was an isolated instance of strange and horrific visions. There are locusts with men's faces, women's hair, and lions' teeth, horses pouring fire and smoke and brimstone out of their mouths, a woman 'clothed with the sun and the moon under her feet', another sitting on a scarlet beast with seven heads and ten horns, a serpent pouring water out of its mouth like a river, and countless cosmic catastrophes, plagues and famines. In the struggle between light and darkness, goodness and evil, which is the theme of the book, the central character on one side is a slain lamb with seven horns and seven eyes, and on the other one of the main figures is a beast who speaks like a dragon and has a mysterious number, 666. Small wonder that faithful Christians have been worried and the Church (as we shall see below) dubious about including the book in the New Testament at all, and uncertain for many centuries as to its correct interpretation. The uncertainty can be illustrated by the views of different periods as to who was the Beast (Antichrist) and Babylon. At the Reformation those who rebelled against the corruption of the church said that the Pope was Antichrist, following certain strains of thought which had begun to appear in the Middle Ages, particularly in heretical circles. Roman Catholics, in reply, found that the number 666 signified Luther. Again at the time of the ferment caused by the meteoric career of Napoleon and especially his dramatic return for one hundred days before Waterloo, many thought that 666 stood for him. More recently both the Kaiser and Adolf Hitler have been candidates for the identification. In the Reformation controversies, the Jesuits, the leading champions of the counter-Reformation, hit upon the true interpretation and the one that was crystal clear to the early Church. Antichrist was not Christian Rome, but the pagan Rome which had begun persecuting the Church. A vital point hangs on this, that the immediate fulfilment of the book is to be looked for not in the future but in the past. This point of view won its way slowly, until it was clinched by the discovery of many other examples of literature in a similar style, which is known as 'apocalyptic'.[1] It meant that Revelation was no longer in a class by itself. Comparable literature existed, and from it the clue to the interpretation of apocalyptic writing could be discovered. The work of scholars in the last hundred years has put us in a far better position to understand John's book than any other generation of Christians since he wrote, and we should thank God for their work.

Revelation is not the only apocalyptic writing in the Bible; there is the book of Daniel in the Old Testament and there are apocalyptic passages in the prophetical books such as Isa. 24 to 27 and Ezek. 38 and 39. These were not recognised as such, but were merged in prophecy, because prophecy was thought of primarily as the detailed foretelling of the future rather than the discerning of 'the signs of the times', or the declaring of God's will for the prophet's own generation. Consequently apocalyptic was not recognised. Daniel, for instance, was thought of as a detailed prophecy of Israel's future, written during the exile in Babylon (586-

[1] 'The simplest reader can, without too much difficulty, understand the Gospels and Acts; the most learned cannot, without some special training in Jewish literature, understand the Revelation of St. John.' *The New Testament Letters*, Prefaced and Paraphrased, by J. W. C. Wand, London, 1946 (from the Introduction, p. viii).

536 B.C.), whereas in fact it was a tract for the times, written when the Jews were undergoing the first of the many *religious* persecutions they have suffered in their history (see p. 39). Antiochus Epiphanēs, king of Syria, who controlled the country, tried to introduce Greek customs and suppress the Jewish religion. In 166 B.C. he erected a heathen altar in the Temple at Jerusalem, and Jewish resistance began under Judas Maccabeus, his father, and his brothers. The Book of Daniel was written to encourage this, and in the guise of prophecy gives a pretty accurate account of Jewish history from the exile to that moment, whereupon it suddenly becomes vague. In the author's view the historical process would culminate after the overthrow of Antiochus in the setting up of the Kingdom of the Saints of the Most High. It is very suitable to quote Daniel because John was greatly influenced by it, and pursues much the same technique in description—we find he uses the same mysterious beast-like figures—and has a similar view of history. To John, the persecuting Roman Empire will shortly be overthrown and the history of the present earth will end with the reign of Christ for 1,000 years, after which there would be a new heaven and a new earth and 'the former things would pass away'. Just as in Daniel Nebuchadnezzàr stands for Antiochus Epiphanēs, so in Revelation Babylon stands for Rome. What has helped us to understand this has been the discovery of about thirty apocalypses which had been lost. Doubtless in time more will turn up. One (2 Esdras, sometimes called 4 Esdras) has been in our Apocrypha all along, but although it is important, as it was mostly written about the same time as Revelation, it has not attracted much attention. A good account of most of them is to be found in R. H. Charles's volume in the Home University Library, *Between the Old and New Testaments*. The most important is the Book of Enoch, which is explicitly quoted in the New Testament (Jude vv. 14 and 15) and which is published in an English translation (in common with several others) by the S.P.C.K.[1] It undoubtedly influenced the mind of John and

[1] Details from the S.P.C.K., Northumberland Avenue, London, W.C.2.

has affected Revelation. There were also other Christian apocalypses, but they are not of much importance. They can be found in *The Apocryphal New Testament* edited by M. R. James (O.U.P.).

3. Characteristics of Apocalyptic Literature

'Apocalypse' is a Greek word; from the Latin translation of it comes our word 'revelation'. The sense is that of 'unveiling' some truth which has hitherto been hidden. The word occurs in the New Testament in this sense, e.g. in Rom. 8. 19, 'the earnest expectation of the creation waiteth for the revealing of the sons of God'. Revelation is so supreme an example of the type that it is frequently called The Apocalypse. Prophecy, as we can tell from our Bibles, practically came to an end within a century of the return from Exile (Malachi); that was why John the Baptist caused such a sensation, for he appeared to be a return to the prophetic tradition. Jewish thought developed in three ways in the three centuries before Jesus: (1) in the elaboration of the unwritten law; (2) in the 'Wisdom' literature, of which our best examples are Ecclesiasticus and the Book of Wisdom itself, both in the Apocrypha; (3) in apocalyptic. This last was the latest. The oppression of Antiochus Epiphanēs seems to have started it, and it persisted until after the failure of the last of the Jewish revolts against Rome, that of Bar Cochba in A.D. 135. It has been called 'Tracts for Bad Times', and seems peculiar to the Jewish religion. It grew out of the prophetic view of God's control over the doings of nations and peoples in human history, but differed from it in various respects.

(*a*) It despaired of the earth, and held that things would go from bad to worse until God finally intervened to punish wrongdoing and establish his Kingdom. This would be in the immediate future, and was usually to be accomplished by some heavenly figure, some transcendent Messiah.

(*b*) It was a literary production unlike the verbal oracles of most Hebrew prophecy.

(*c*) It was pseudonymous, as were Daniel or Enoch, and usually took the name of some hero of the past, partly to secure authority and partly because of the danger of the message it stood for.

(*d*) It abounded in weird symbolism, mythological beasts and the like, again because it was underground resistance literature. These symbols were perfectly clear to the readers though they often puzzle us.

(*e*) It believed in life after death, as against the traditional Hebrew belief in a shadowy existence in *she'ol*, the underworld.

Apocalyptic literature was always considered unorthodox by the leading Jews, though it suited the mood of an occupied country which detested its Roman overlords. It was particularly popular in Galilee, which had only been Judaised a comparatively short time and was far from orthodox (cf. 'Can there any good thing come out of Nazareth?' John 1. 46). After the fall of Jerusalem to the Romans in A.D. 70 the Jewish religion was preserved by the Rabbis, who did not regard apocalyptic favourably. The leading ideas which led to Bar Cochba's revolt and failure confirmed them in this. So did the fact that Christians had taken it up. It has therefore faded out of Jewish religion. The history of Christian apocalyptic was similar. Revelation is thoroughly in the style of apocalyptic writing. From the Roman point of view it was seditious literature; for the Christian author and reader it was dangerous. We may think it obscure, but its meaning would be only too plain to John's Christian contemporaries. Babylon the harlot, the city that reigned over the kings of the earth (17. 18), can only be Rome, and the Beast on which she sits the Imperial system. It suited the mood of Christians when the Empire was indulging in its bouts of persecution, but was less welcome when Christianity became influential, recognised by the State and respectable. A century or so later Tertullian, the great scholar and lawyer of the Western Church, was to assure the Emperor that Antichrist was not Rome, but a rival power that would take her place. Meanwhile faithful Christians prayed for Rome, who kept Antichrist at bay. Hence the Church was extremely doubtful as to whether to admit the book into the 'canon', or 'rule', of Scripture at all.

The process by which the canon of the New Testament came to be settled was a very gradual one, and no precise date can be given when it was completed. By about the beginning of the fifth century A.D. it was pretty clear which books the Church was prepared to recognise as authoritative. Revelation was one of the books about which there were most doubts, partly because of difficulties about the authorship (*see below*), and partly because of its weird style and the fact that the secret of apocalyptic had been lost. The Christians of the Eastern Mediterranean were particularly doubtful; the Apocalypse hardly seems to have reached the Syriac-speaking churches at all, for it is present in only one MS. of their Bible. The West tended to accept it, though Jerome had doubts. In the end, largely owing to the influence of Athanasius, it was accepted in the canon.

But acceptance did not mean that it was understood. The key had been lost. It has been left for recent generations to realise what the early Church had understood, that Revelation was written for its time. We are now in a position to strengthen our faith and hear God speaking to us through John's work, unencumbered by the confusions which have afflicted ordinary Christians and commentators for centuries and which caused unnecessary difficulties even to one of the greatest British theologians of the last century, F. D. Maurice in his *Lectures on the Apocalypse* of 1860. As E. F. Scott says, the difficulties that remain are puzzles rather than problems, and Revelation has ceased to be a mysterious book as it was to our fathers. 'In some respects it is now the simplest and most intelligible of all New Testament writings, for the general meaning of it lies on the surface, and it offers few of those deep religious problems which we encounter in the Gospels and in the Epistles of Paul.' (*op. cit.*, p. 20.)

4. The Contents of the Apocalypse

Since the book is so completely unknown to so many Christians, and bearing in mind that those who do try to read it through in one sitting to get a broad impression of it tend only to be lost in a confused series of chaotic images, it is worth while to give a short synopsis of the Apocalypse, dividing it into the sections which will be taken together in the commentary. This is the more necessary as the A.V. has no paragraphs to indicate the progress of the narrative.

1. 1-3   Solemn introduction.
   4-8   Greetings, and the offering of praise to the risen Christ.
   9-20   John's account of his command to write the book and his vision of the risen Christ.
2. 1-7   Letter to the Church in Ephesus.
   8-11   Letter to the Church in Smyrna.
   12-17   Letter to the Church in Pergamum.
   18-29   Letter to the Church in Thyatira.
3. 1-6   Letter to the Church in Sardis
   7-13   Letter to the Church in Philadelphia
   14-22   Letter to the Church in Laodicea
4. 1-11   Vision of God in heaven as Creator with twenty-four elders and four beasts (R.V. living creatures) offering a doxology of praise to him.
5. 1-8   Vision of Christ in heaven as Redeemer, 'a Lamb standing as it had been slain,' who by being worthy to open the book with the seven seals takes upon himself the completion of the judgments of the world, and is offered a doxology of praise together with God the Creator.
6. 1-8   The first four of the seven seals are opened, letting loose the 'four horsemen of the Apocalypse' who bring disasters on the world.
   9-11   The opening of the fifth seal discloses the souls of the slain Christians asking how long judgment of the wicked is to be delayed.
   12-17   Further disasters follow upon the opening of the sixth seal.

7.	1-8	The sealing of the 144,000 servants of God.
	9-17	Vision of the future glorious destiny before the throne of God of those who came out of great tribulation and washed their robes in the blood of the Lamb.
8.	1-13	The opening of the seventh seal leads, after half-an-hour's silence in heaven, to the sounding of four out of seven trumpets, each of which is the signal for further cataclysms.
9.	1-11	The fifth trumpet-sound is the prelude to an invasion of fearsome locusts from the abyss; this is also the first of three woes.
	12-21	At the sound of the sixth trumpet two hundred million horsemen appear, bringing a threefold plague: this is the second of the woes (cf. 11. 14).
10.	1-11	A strong angel gives John a very little book to swallow; he is also told not to write down another series of visions, 'the seven thunders'.
11.	1-13	John is told to measure the Temple of God at Jerusalem; a story follows of two witnesses who prophecy there, are killed by a Beast from the abyss, and rise again after three and a half days and ascend to heaven.
	14-19	The seventh trumpet sounds and a chorus of praise is heard in heaven.
12.	1-6	Vision of a woman in labour whose child is caught up to heaven to escape a dragon waiting to devour it.
	7-12	War in heaven in which Michael and his angels cast out the dragon and his angels to earth.
	13-17	The dragon persecutes the woman (who flees into the wilderness) and makes war 'on the rest of her seed'.

13. 1-10	The dragon calls a Beast from the sea and gives him his authority; the Beast makes war on 'the saints' and overcomes them. (This is apparently the third woe.)
11-18	A second Beast comes—from the earth this time—and exercises the authority of the first; the faithless are given the mark of the Beast and the faithful are killed; the Beast's number is 666 (later this Beast becomes the false prophet, e.g. 16. 13 and 19. 20).
17. 1-5	Vision of the Lamb and the 144,000 on Mount Sion.
6-20	A series of angels expatiate on the judgment of Babylon (Rome) and the followers of the Beast; the vintage of the earth is gathered and cast into the winepress of the wrath of God.
15. 2-4	The entire martyred host in heaven sings the song of Moses and the Lamb.
1, 5-8	The third series of plagues, the seven vials (bowls, R.V.).
16. 1-21	The seven vials are poured out and are followed by further disasters, including the fall of Babylon (Rome).
17. 1-18	Further account of the fall of Babylon, pictured now as a great harlot sitting upon the Beast. The Beast finally makes war on her.
18. 1-24	Paean of triumph over the fall of Babylon, the great harlot.
19. 1-10	Heaven rejoices at the marriage of the Lamb.
11-16	The fifth horseman of the Apocalypse: The Word of God.
17-21	The final battle; the Beast and the false prophet are cast into the lake of fire.
20. 1-3	Satan bound in the abyss for 1,000 years.
4-6	The Millennium and the first resurrection.

INTRODUCTION

7-10	Satan loosed, devoured by fire as he besieges 'the beloved city' with his armies, and cast into the lake of fire together with the Beast and the false prophet.
11-15	The last judgment; death and Hades cast into the lake of fire.
21 – 22. 5	Visions of the new Jerusalem and the new heaven and new earth.
22. 6-21	Final statements and messages of John.

Our task now is to sort this apparently heterogeneous collection of narratives, visions and songs of praise into a framework which will give the whole some kind of orderly sequence. One of the easiest aspects to grasp is the skilful way in which John has produced violent contrasts by switching the scene from heaven to earth, or—to express it in another way—from scenes of grace to scenes of judgment, so that the masses of light and shade stand out as in an Arthur Wragg drawing, and the whole book has been called 'a study in contrasts'. Thus we can readily appreciate the artistry with which he builds up the suspense, through the series of plagues, by his contrasts.

Various commentators have devised different divisions of the whole book, e.g. some into three, some into seven sections. They differ among themselves, and there is no certainty that any of them was present in John's mind, though in view of his preference for sevens a sevenfold division has the most plausibility. Our practical problem is to arrive at a division which will help us to grasp the flow of the narrative beneath the apparent diversity of the contents. In fact, the earlier and later chapters are fairly clear; the difficulty comes in the middle ones. Leaving the details of these aside for the moment, we get the following simple scheme:—

1. The Prologue (ch.1).
2. Letters to the seven churches (ch. 2 and 3).
3. The vision of heaven (ch. 4 and 5).
4. The three series of Judgments—seals, trumpets, and vials (ch. 6 – 16).
5. The fall of Rome (ch. 17 – 20. 3).

6. The Millennial City (ch. 20. 4-10, and 21. 7 – 22. 2, 14, 15).
7. The Last Judgment (ch. 20. 11-15).
8. The Eternal City (ch. 21. 1-6, and 22. 3-5).
9. Epilogue (ch. 22. 6-13 and 16-21).

There are certain difficulties in the last three chapters of Revelation which call for this rearrangement of the material in sections 6, 7, 8, and 9; these will be dealt with in the commentary. For the moment we can be content with this fairly straightforward guide to the broad divisions of the book. Leaving aside the Prologue and Epilogue, it is a sevenfold division. But it is still necessary to unravel the complicated middle chapters in section 4. The best way of doing so is to separate the three series of judgments, and it then becomes clear that there are four parenthetical sections inserted in the midst of them:—

4. The three series of Judgments (ch. 6 – 16).
   (*a*) The seven seals (ch. 6)
        1st parenthesis—The marking of the saints and the ultimate triumph of the redeemed (ch. 7)
   (*b*) The seven trumpets (ch. 8 – 9; 11. 14-19; 13)
        2nd parenthesis—The angel of the book; the temple and the two witnesses (ch. 10 – 11. 13)
   The seven trumpets, continued (ch. 11. 14-19)
        3rd parenthesis—the woman, the child, and the dragon (ch. 12)
   The seven trumpets, continued (ch. 13)
        4th parenthesis—vision of the Lamb on Mount Sion and of the Son of Man in power (ch. 14)
   (*c*) The seven vials (bowls) (ch. 15 – 16)

Analysing it in this fashion we find that the heart of the difficulties in following the thread is reduced to ch. 10 – 14 where a parenthetic vision interrupts the narrative after the sounding of the sixth trumpet and where, after the sounding of the seventh in ch. 11. 14-19, it is hard to see what exactly is parenthetic and what is main narrative (in ch. 12 – 14) until we reach the vials in ch. 15, when all seems plain sailing again. On closer examination ch. 12 is clearly parenthetical, so that we can reduce the confusion to ch. 13 – 14 only. It seems fairly clear that ch. 13 is part of the main narrative, and we have taken it as following on the sounding of the seventh trumpet and as the content of the third woe which is announced in 11. 14 and never explicitly mentioned afterwards. That leaves 14 as the fourth parenthetic vision, the last part of which foreshadows narratives which are to come later in the account of the fall of Rome.

Behind this difficulty of unravelling the main narrative from parentheses lies the question as to whether John was intending to write a narrative sequence at all, or whether he meant to record a series of parallel visions; whether, for instance, the three series of judgments are in sequence or different accounts of the same thing. On the whole, it is difficult to resist the impression of movement which the narrative gives, but we have to remember that John varies his technique, partly by inserting his visions into the scenes of judgment, partly by giving foretastes of what he is going to deal with again later, so that his thought often moves spirally. That is why we get the parentheses. Fortunately it is the beginning and end of the book which matter most for the ordinary reader, and here the difficulties are less. The commentary will therefore concentrate rather more on these parts than on the middle section.

5. Who wrote Revelation?

The answer must be simply—John. All we know about him is what he tells us about himself in the first chapter. He does not claim to be an apostle or an elder, but a prophet and a 'brother and companion in tribulation, and in the kingdom and patience of Jesus Christ' (1. 3, 9). There is no solid ground for the tradition that the author is the Apostle John. He is certainly not the author of the Fourth Gospel. The authorship of the Fourth Gospel is itself a thorny problem, but we can at least say that the books are not by the same person. This was pointed out long ago by Dionysius of Alexandria, who was a pupil of the Alexandrian scholar Origen and who died in A.D. 265. Not only are the ideas of the two books very different but their styles are even more antithetic. Of the 900 or so words in both books they have fewer than half in common. The Gospel tends to stress just those aspects of the Christian faith which Revelation neglects. They have indeed certain features in common (for instance, their interpretation of the death of Christ), but this is hardly surprising as both probably came from the same part of Asia Minor, and in any case both are Christian books. R. H. Charles has shown conclusively that the Greek style of Revelation is quite unique, 'unlike any Greek that was ever penned by mortal man' (see below, pp. 42-3). Obviously John was a Jewish Christian who thought in Aramaic (the dialect of Hebrew that was spoken in our Lord's time, as Hebrew had become by then a dead language), and had never mastered the Greek of his day, but wrote in a kind of Hebraic Greek. Before settling in Asia Minor (the island of Patmos where he was imprisoned is just off the coast of Asia Minor) he may well have come from somewhere like Galilee. The style is the same throughout, so the book is a unity, John having worked over and written out his dreams and visions in his waking hours. Unlike Jewish apocalypses, it is not pseudonymous, but under his own name. It seems to have a certain undefined authority, probably owing to the inherent weight of his character and views, so that he does not need to present any credentials.[1]

His thought is saturated in the Old Testament. Out of 404 verses there are 518 Old Testament references and countless echoes; there are no direct quotations. The prophetic books have particularly influenced him, especially Isaiah, Jeremiah, Ezekiel, and Daniel; Zechariah is the most quoted of the minor prophets. Psalms and Exodus are also prominent. There are echoes of New Testament books, especially of Matthew, Luke, 1 Thessalonians, 1 and 2 Corinthians, Colossians, Ephesians, and Hebrews. John knows both the

[1] It has been suggested, e.g. by Prof. J. H. Michael (*Expository Times*, May 1948) that John wrote a Jewish Apocalypse in his (supposed) pre-Christian days, and changed it to a Christian one by a few additions after he had been converted to Christianity. There is no need of this hypothesis. An examination of John's ideas and methods of using the O.T. and other sources, which follows in the later sections of this Introduction, shows that John's Christian understanding controlled the use of his materials throughout.

Hebrew and the Greek versions of the Old Testament (the latter is known as the Septuagint and referred to by the symbol LXX), as well as the apocalypses in Greek, such as Enoch.

6. When was Revelation written?

A.D. 95 – 96 is the most likely date, as one of the early Fathers of the Church, Irenaeus, said (c. A.D. 180). This was the last year of the Emperor Domitian, when he began a persecution of Christians, the first to extend to Asia, where the cult of Emperor-worship flourished. Nero's persecution thirty years previously had been localised in Rome. Vespasian, the previous Emperor (except for the short reign of Titus), had not taken his divinity very seriously, but Domitian did. He insisted on state officials calling him 'our Lord and God' and had a cousin executed and a niece and several others banished for refusing as Christians to take part in Emperor-worship. From the point of view of the authorities, Emperor-worship was an entirely reasonable thing as an effort to bind the empire together by the one thing needful which it lacked, a common religion. The Japanese adopted the same policy recently. After all, the Emperor was far more august and had far more power than any of the petty gods who were widely worshipped. But to the Christian it was utterly impossible and blasphemous to worship a man, however august. This is what gives its sense of crisis to John's book. A 'no compromise' issue had arisen, the outcome of which would mean death for the Christians. It could only be avoided by apostasy, by publicly throwing incense on one of the altars to the Emperor. A similar situation arose not so long ago in Nazi-controlled countries when Christians were asked to exclude believers who were of Jewish blood from their fellowship. To compromise would mean apostasy.

Faced with this crisis John saw the decisive battle between good and evil in the world as set. He had no doubt, as we shall see, of its triumphant outcome, even though the martyrdom of all Christians was involved. His conviction that things were moving to a final crisis was sharpened by two events in his own lifetime. One was the fall of Jerusalem in

A.D. 70 to the Roman armies. An echo of this is found in our Gospels (Luke 21. 2ff.). Even to a Jew who was a Christian, like John, the overthrow of the 'holy city, which spiritually is called Sodom and Egypt, where also their Lord was crucified' (Rev. 11. 8), would seem of quite fundamental significance, a sign that God's judgments were abroad in the earth. That is why he incorporates, in ch. 11 of Revelation, what is probably an earlier vision of Jerusalem. The other event was the sudden revelation of the feet of clay of the Roman colossus, when there were three pretenders to the throne in one year between the death of Nero in A.D. 68 and the accession of Vespasian in A.D. 69. This showed that the vast and apparently unshakeable empire could yet be rocked to its foundations. Again God's judgments were abroad. John appears to include in Revelation, notably in the letters to the seven churches of ch. 2 and 3, material which comes from an earlier time such as that of Vespasian.

Connected with this turmoil in the empire was the widespread belief that Nero would return from the dead, and this gives rise to some of the most mysterious passages of Revelation, which would baffle us entirely if we had not the clue to this legend. Nero killed himself in a house outside Rome in A.D. 68. Soon after a rumour sprang up that he was not dead but that he had fled to the Parthians (on the east frontier of the empire) and would return at the head of the Parthian army. Pretenders to the throne claimed to be Nero, and one was supported by the Parthians. Later, when it became less and less probable that he was alive, the legend changed to the belief that he would return from the underworld. Difficult as it is for us to take this seriously, there is no doubt that it was a widespread belief in John's day. It is to this that he refers in 13. 3 and in 17. 11: 'the Beast that was and is not and is to come'. The mysterious number 666 is the cryptogram of the words Neron Kesar in Hebrew. To John the world is in a ferment, and the widespread persecution of the Christians in Asia and the blasphemous claim to divine honours by Domitian is a sign of the imminent climax of history. Just as the author of Daniel foreshortens his perspective and sees the Kingdom of the Saints of the Most

High being set up immediately after the overthrow of Antiochus Epiphanēs, so John expects the millennium and the end of the world to follow upon the imminent overthrow of Rome. Nero is to return as the exactor of divine judgment upon Babylon (Rome). But, having overthrown her with his Parthian armies, he would in turn be overthrown by the returning Christ at the head of His armies in the final conflict of good and evil in the world. Nero is a ghastly counterpart of the returning Messiah. John is in the full apocalyptic tradition.

7. Leading Ideas of Revelation

Most of these will become clear in the course of the commentary itself. It will be sufficiently obvious by now that much of the mystifying symbolism is conventional in apocalyptic and would present no puzzles to John's readers. Some of it indeed is derived from Persian and pagan sources of which both he and his readers were quite unaware but which have been uncovered today. Nevertheless, Beasts, angels, and cosmic portents would immediately remind them, for example, of Daniel or Ezekiel. They would also probably know many of the books which had not been accepted into the 'canon' of Jewish Scripture, such as Enoch, which influenced John. Antichrist would be a familiar figure, and the woes which were associated with the Messiah commonplace. Numbers would not worry them: they would know that 3 is the number of heaven, 4 of earth, 7 the perfect number and 12 and its multiples symbols of completeness, and that 'the time and times and half a time' $(1+2+\frac{1}{2}=3\frac{1}{2}$ years), which also appears as 1260 days or 42 months, stands for the period of supremacy of evil.

Moreover, when we appreciate the literary problem which faced John it is difficult to see how he could tackle it in any other way. That problem was how to portray the Last Things, the end of history. The Greeks never had to solve this problem, because they believed that history repeats itself in endless cycles. Neither had the eastern religions, for whom history is meaningless. In modern times the Marxist has attempted a solution by talking of the classless society after the revolution, when the state will wither away; concepts which, when thought about, are clearly as mythological as those of John and have the disadvantage that they do not imply that there is anything evil in the historical process on which divine judgment has to be passed. Marxists do not realise that history by itself cannot redeem itself. The only other modern attempt to express the Last Things is that of certain scientists who do not realise what they are doing, but look to a wonderful harmony in the future by the rational application of science to everyday life. This, too, fails to understand the depth of human evil and the inability of scientific categories to cope with the human spirit and personality.

Against these, John's picture, rooted as it is in the profound Hebrew apocalyptic and prophetic belief in a God of righteousness and mercy who is both transcendent and immanent, has great advantages. John has used symbols to describe the end of the world which express the following truths: (1) That God is in control of history and has the initiative; (2) that there is a real struggle in history between good and evil; (3) that the supreme clue to the understanding of God's character, actions, and purpose is to be found in the life, death, and resurrection of Jesus of Nazareth, and that these events have a direct bearing on everything that happens in history; (4) that the struggle will go on to the end of time and that no power in history itself can cure the evil: 'both grow together until harvest'; (5) therefore God himself must in the end cope with evil, and history be 'swallowed up in eternity'; (6) heaven is the most real place and state of all.

We do not know how history will end; whether, for example, the earth will get colder or hotter. Either way, life will cease, and scientists seem divided as to which is the more likely. The spiritual truth involved is the same in either case. In any event it is impossible to express the end of the world, when time comes to an end, in other symbols than those of a poetic or mythological character. The same is true of the beginning of the world, as the creation narratives in Genesis show. We have to take words whose associations are linked to the world of time and space in which we live, and use them to suggest the end of these dimensions. The Jews learned to do this in apocalyptic, and no better way has yet been found. If we find it strange, it is because we have not thought about the problem, and a whole range of Biblical truth, including matters of decisive moment for the Christian, are closed to us. The sooner we face them the better.

John, of course, was wrong in expecting the immediate downfall of Rome and with it the overthrow of all evil powers that withstand God, though his expectations may well have seemed plausible at the time. Antichrist did not succeed Domitian, but five good Emperors under whom there was general prosperity. No more than Daniel's was his prophecy literally fulfilled, or that of Paul, who for a good part of his life certainly expected to see the end of the world (1 Thess. 4. 16 f.). Yet that is not the important point about Revelation. Apocalyptic writers were expressing more than they realised by their manner of writing, as did the High Priest who said it was expedient that one man should die for the people (John 11. 50). Rome as an empire did fall 350 years later, and by an extraordinary irony Rome as a city became the new holy city of the Church. Yet history did not come to an end, and every attempt to push the date forward on the basis of calculations drawn from Revelation has ended in a fiasco. Again that is not the point. The real point is that the end of history can hardly be described in any other way than by that of John, and that the principles he portrays are the fundamental truths behind the universe. Tyranny does always defeat itself; the cause of Christ in the end will be victorious; God does and will bring good out of evil; and the faithfulness of Christian witness in all circumstances, even unto death, is not in vain, but is an essential element in the divine victory.

8. Is Revelation a Christian Book?

Almost all we have said in the previous section could apply equally to a Jewish as to a Christian apocalypse. Is Revelaation really a Christian book? Was the Church right to include it in the canon? Many have doubted it. Consider a recent unfavourable verdict from Professor C. H. Dodd's *The Apostolic Preaching and its Developments*:[1]

'The whole apparatus of Jewish apocalyptic is here adapted to Christian use. In cryptic imagery the writer refers to current and immediately impending events, the political conflicts of the time, the Parthian menace, the fear of a return of Nero, the growth of Caesar worship, and the intensification of persecution—interprets these as the infallible signs of the approaching advent of the Lord. The whole emphasis falls upon that which is to come.

'The other elements in the *kerygma* [i.e. the content of the early Christian preaching] are indeed present as a background. The death and resurrection of the Lord are presupposed as the condition of his ultimate triumph and he is seen in vision walking in the midst of golden candlesticks, which are churches. But all this is subordinated to the intense expectation of glory yet to come which absorbed the writer's real interest. And, if we review the book as a whole, we must judge that this excessive emphasis on the future has the effect of relegating to a secondary place just those elements of the Gospel which are most distinctive of Christianity—the faith that in the finished work of Christ God has already acted for the salvation of man, and the blessed sense of living in the divine presence here and now.

'Under the influence of this revived Jewish eschatology, [i.e. doctrine of the Last Things] Christianity was in danger of falling back into the position of the early apocalyptists. Minds dominated by the fantastic visions of the Revelation of John might easily lose the sense that all had been made new by the coming of Christ and that in the communion of his people the life of the age to come was a present possession through the spirit which he had given . . . The effects of this relapse into pre-christian eschatology are evident in the tone and temper of Revelation itself. With all the magnificence of its imagery and the splendour of its visions of the majesty of God and the world to come, we are bound to judge that in its conception of the character of God and his attitude to man the book falls far below the level not only

[1] p. 86 ff. (1936 edition).

of the teaching of Jesus but of the best parts of the Old Testament. Our Lord's proclamation of the Kingdom of God was associated with a new conception of the infinite lovingkindness of the heavenly Father. It was "a new teaching, with authority". Where shall we find its echoes in the Revelation of John? At most, in a verse or two here and there. The God of the Apocalypse can hardly be recognised as the Father of our Lord Jesus Christ, nor has the fierce Messiah, whose warriors ride in blood up to their horses' bridles, many traits that could recall Him of whom the primitive *kerygma* proclaimed that He went about doing good and healing all who were oppressed by the devil because God was with Him.'

That is the case against Revelation put very well. There is much in it. No doubt there was a tendency in the early Church, steeped as it was in the current Messianic expectation which our Lord so rudely disappointed, not to be content with the full majesty of his finished work and to look for a second coming on more familiar lines which would redress the balance of the first, when

> Those that set at nought and sold him,
>   Deeply wailing,
> Shall the true Messiah see.' [1]

John is not free from this. It is also true that he appears to be most certain where our Lord was most reticent over the time of the end and the details of the future. This, however, is but the necessary imagery of apocalyptic. More serious, there is scarcely any suggestion that men can be transformed by the power of God, that evil characters can be remade (21. 24 and 22. 2 are the only exceptions). In John's view the division between black and white is absolute. The effects of the judgments on the ungodly is akin to that of the plagues on Pharaoh. The only thing that can happen to the wicked is their destruction. There is no trace of the mind of Jesus who prayed, 'Father, forgive them, for they know not what they do', for those who nailed him to the cross, and bade his followers, 'Pray for them that despitefully use you'.

[1] Cf. Rev. 1. 7.

There is scarcely a trace of the Jesus of the synoptic gospels. It is here that John chiefly fails, not so much in making the issue black and white, for we see that at times it does in fact become black and white, and in his particular case, no matter what benefits the Roman empire gave to men, if the Emperor claimed to be God the issue was clear-cut. His failure is in his attitude to the sinful.

But when that has been said and it has been admitted that the *whole* gospel is not to be found in Revelation, what glories remain! The work of Christ is not so much a background, as Professor Dodd asserts, but is the centre. Nowhere in the New Testament is Jesus given higher honour than he is in Revelation. Indeed identical worship is given to him as to the Father (cf. ch. 5). When we stop to think what this must have meant for a Jew with his strictly monotheistic background, we see what a sure grasp John has on the centrality of Christ. It was precisely as a result of this sure grasp expressed by men like John that the church was driven slowly and haltingly in the next three hundred and fifty years to work out the doctrine of the Holy Trinity. In Revelation John uses all the resources of his art to express in symbol and picture-form the supreme work of Jesus culminating in his death and resurrection, truths that were expressed more historically and theologically in other parts of the New Testament, e.g. in Paul's Epistles. Here the victorious followers of the 'Lamb that had been slain' can join in a *new* song of deliverance as participators in his victory, the song of Moses and the Lamb. Further, titles of honour which in the Old Testament are applied to Yahweh (Jehovah) are applied in Revelation to Jesus, e.g. 'Lord of Lords' (Deut. 10. 17), 'the first and the last' (Isa. 44. 6). Indeed, it is only because of the advent of the risen and ascended Messiah in heaven that the intensity of the conflict with Satanic evil on earth is brought to a head (see p. 93). The Lamb whose wrath plays such a part in the pages of the book is one who has been sprinkled with his *own* blood, not that of his enemies. He is triumphant through *self*-sacrifice. Therefore he is worthy to be the bearer of God's judgments, *and it is that thought which lies behind the judgments of the*

Lamb. Here, and this is a crucial point, Revelation breaks decisively with the Old Testament and has its feet firmly within the Christian dispensation. The judgments of God are not vengeful but spring from 'the impossible mercy of giving us the blessing of the light which we hate' (F. D. Maurice, op. cit. p. 13) and illustrate the principle laid down in the fourth gospel (John 3. 16-19) that the condemnation is because 'light came into the world and men loved darkness rather than light, because their deeds were evil'.

Nor does John ignore the present joys of the Christian life, though his view of the imminent crisis does not allow him to develop it as it is developed in other parts of the New Testament. The Church is put into the very closest relation with her Lord. She is the bride of Christ (cf. Eph. 5. 21ff.), she is what the old Israel failed to be, a kingdom of priests; the Christians are the true Jews who have fulfilled the vocation which the Jews by race failed to do; the new Jerusalem will have not only the names of the tribes of Israel on the gates but those of the apostles on its foundations. Loyalty to him who stands at the door and knocks is the one requisite of the Christian. 'He who overcometh' is the one name that is given to the Christian in the whole book. The offering of praise to God in an overpowering sense of joy and thanksgiving for what he has done through the Lamb is seen as the final destiny and profoundest activity of the faithful Christian. But the unsurpassed visions of the reality of heaven must not blind us to the present power possessed by the Christian as he is watched and guarded in the midst of evils which, though they may be powerful enough to kill the body, yet are not able to harm the soul.

Lastly, what of the fate of the wicked? The general drift of the book (though there are possible exceptions in 20. 10 and 24. 11) is that in the last resort continual opposition to God's love means spiritual annihilation; the personality as such ceases to exist. Its fate is destruction. Death and Hades are cast into the lake of fire (20. 14), and fire annihilates. Pictures of eternal torments which have been popular have gone far beyond any Biblical evidence and are mostly contrary to it. Whether any soul will in fact finally resist God, we cannot say. We know that 'it is a fearful thing to fall into the hands of the living God' (Heb. 10. 31), and we can also say, 'We will fall into the hands of the Lord and not into the hands of men: for as his majesty is so also is his mercy' (Ecclus. 2 .17).

9. The Old Testament in the Book of Revelation

No one who knows anything about the Old Testament can fail to notice how big a part it plays in Revelation. You have only to run your eye down the columns of a Bible with cross-references to see how densely studded our author's work is with Old Testament echoes. The Old Testament is, in fact, his main source, and again and again one has to go back to the Old Testament in order to understand his meaning. Almost any passage would illustrate this; we may take ch. 4. as a convenient example. In that chapter 'the throne set in heaven' in verse 2 is an echo of Ps. 11. 4; 'the jasper and the sardine stone' in verse 3 come from Ezek. 28. 13; the rainbow is an echo of Ezek. 1. 28; the 'seven lamps of fire' in verse 5, of Ezek. 1. 27; while 'the seven spirits of God' bring us back to Isa. 11. 2. The 'four beasts' of verse 6 are from Ezek. 1 (the major source for this chapter); and the cry they utter, 'Holy, holy, holy', is from Isa. 6. 3. One could trace other fainter echoes of the Old Testament in this chapter, but this is sufficient to show how deeply impregnated our author was with the only scriptures which he knew.

This raises the question: Why did John use the Old Testament so much? The best way to answer such a question is to try to see *how* he uses it; indeed, if we can understand something of his method, we shall be in a fair way towards understanding his central message, for it is true of the author of Revelation, as it is of all the New Testament writers, that what he has to say about the Old Testament is very closely bound up with what he has to say about God.

It would seem at first sight that John's method of dealing with the Old Testament is just to take it over in large or small fragments and incorporate it into his narrative. One can point to many passages where one is instantly reminded of some Old Testament parallel, and often when one looks it up one finds that whole phrases and sentences and almost verses have been echoed. (As a matter of fact, it is well worth noting that we cannot find any examples of whole verses taken over. One of the most remarkable things about John is his technique of quotation. He was no slavish copyist and he re-arranges and manipulates his Old Testament material to suit his own purposes.) We have taken six passages from different parts of the book where the Old Testament element is particularly prominent, and will examine them as an indication of John's use of the Old Testament.

(1) 1. 12-18: We have here a description of a supernatural being who appears to John on Patmos. Nearly all the details are taken from Daniel: the phrase 'one like unto a Son of Man' is from Dan. 7. 13; the description of his garment is mostly from Dan. 10. 5, 6; the detail of his hair being 'white as wool' comes from Dan. 7. 9; and the description of his voice as like 'the sound of many waters' is from Ezek. 43. 2; his pronouncement 'I am the first and the last' echoes Isa. 41.4.

(2) 11. 1: John is given 'a reed like unto a rod' and is told to measure the temple of God. This detail is taken from the fortieth chapter of Ezekiel, where an angel measures the temple in Ezekiel's sight. The same thing happens in Zech. 2. 1.

(3) 13: Most of the incidents in this chapter can be paralleled in Daniel, on which the chapter is plainly modelled. A Beast rising from the sea, the description of the Beast, the blasphemies which he utters, all come from Dan. 7. The setting up of an image for all men to worship is no doubt an echo of Nebuchadnezzar's image in Dan. 3.

(4) 18: This chapter is a magnificent taunt-song against Rome, hidden under the traditional name of Babylon. One cannot assign it *en bloc* to any part of the Old Testament; there are many echoes of Isaiah, but the Old Testament passage which it most obviously echoes is Ezek. 26 and 27. The forceful detail of the merchant princes bewailing the fate of the great commercial capital comes from there,

as does the catalogue of her wares. Ezekiel's taunt-song was uttered against Tyre, not Babylon.

(5) 19. 11-16; A vision of God's judgment on his enemies. Though it recalls many Old Testament passages, there is one in particular which lies behind it, Isa. 63. 1-6 (see especially Rev. 19. 13, 15; with this passage should be put Rev. 14. 19-20).

(6) 21: The description of the heavenly city constantly brings us back to the later chapters of Isaiah. The new heaven and earth comes from Isa. 65. 17; the picture of the 'bride adorned for her husband' from Isa. 61. 10; in verse 19 of this chapter the notion of the foundations being adorned with precious stones is from Isa. 54. 11. In verse 23 the city has no need of the sun, which is from Isa. 60. 19; and the picture of the saved nations entering the city recalls Isa. 60. 3. As a final example from among others that could be mentioned, with verse 25, where the gates are described as open always, compare Isa. 60. 11.

Now these six passages are only themselves examples of what can be found throughout the book. Admittedly they are conspicuous examples, but they only emphasise the inconspicuous echoes of the Old Testament which are innumerable. The book is soaked in the Old Testament. It is not surprising therefore that some critics have asserted that Revelation is a much more Jewish than Christian book (see p. 30 above). He has just taken over the Old Testament, they have said, unbaptised. This is, however, an entirely superficial criticism: as soon as we examine *how* John uses his Old Testament sources we realise how much of a Christian he is. It is not the fact that he quotes the Old Testament that is significant; it is the context in which he quotes it. We must, then, look at these six passages again, noticing this time *how* he uses his Old Testament sources:

(1) 1. 12-18: We have seen that this passage recalls mostly Daniel, with one echo of Ezekiel and one of Isaiah. But the significant point here is that this passage describes *Jesus Christ*. It is with something of a shock that we recognise in this awe-inspiring Being the 'gentle Jesus' of

the Sunday Schools. His quotation of the Old Testament therefore becomes charged with great meaning, since many of the Old Testament passages quoted refer in their Old Testament context to God himself. This is true of the quotation from Dan. 7. 9, from Ezek. 43. 2 and from Isa. 41. 4. Obviously therefore John, far from slavishly repeating the Old Testament, is actually claiming divine status for the man Jesus Christ. He is also possibly suggesting that the appearance of the angel to Daniel, described in Dan. 10, was in fact an appearance of the pre-existent Christ, but of this we cannot be sure. At least it will be clear that John's use of the Old Testament here has a very definite Christian purpose.

(2) 11. 1: A man measures the temple, a detail taken from Ezekiel. In Ezekiel the action symbolised preservation from harm of the area measured, and presumably was meant by him to signify that the future temple, which he declared would be built after the return of Israel from exile, would be divinely protected. But John must mean something more than this. In his book 'the temple' can only mean one thing: the Temple at Jerusalem had been destroyed. It means 'the temple of the body', and that body is the Body of Christ, the Christian Church. It is a belief often to be found in the New Testament; cf. Mark 14. 57-58; John 2. 19-21; 1 Cor. 6. 19-20. In this little picture, therefore, derived from Ezekiel, John is representing a promise that the members of the Church will be preserved from spiritual harm. The next two passages, Rev. 13 and 18, require separate treatment, so we leave them for the moment and pass on to:

(5) 19. 11-16: We have seen that verses 13 and 15, especially in this passage, recall Isa. 63. 1-6. The Isaiah passage is a terrible, almost a bloodthirsty, picture of God executing judgment on his enemies. He tramples on them in his wrath so that his garments are sprinkled with blood like a man who has been treading the grape vintage. At first sight John seems to be giving us the same picture, with Christ substituted for God. But there are two significant differences: his garment is not 'sprinkled' (Isa. 63. 3) but

dipped (A.V., and R.V. margin; the Greek word is the same root as 'baptised') and he is followed by the 'armies which were in heaven,' no doubt the hosts of triumphant martyrs. The astonishing truth seems to be that here Christ's garment is dipped in his own blood, and the way he has judged and overcome his enemies is by the Cross. The martyrs are frequently described in Revelation as they that *overcome*, and here is a picture of their conquest, which was carried out on the plane of history when they in their turn died a martyr's death. Christ has undergone his baptism of blood (cf. Mark 10. 38), and has thereby conquered his enemies. So John has marvellously transformed what at first sight seems a very 'unchristian' Old Testament passage so as to make it a symbol of the glory and power of the Cross.

(6) 21: Much of this chapter echoes the later chapters of Isaiah. We do not know at what point in Israel's history these chapters were written, but it must have been at times of eclipse and difficulty, for they are full of exhortations to hope for the future, and they describe in beautiful language an ideal state of affairs, where Israel dwells in perfect communion with God and all nations acknowledge her spiritual leadership. John takes these visions and puts them, so to speak, on the other side of God's act in Jesus Christ. Reconciliation between God and man, universal saving knowledge of God, a holy nation destined to spread that knowledge, these are no longer dreams, but have come true in Jesus Christ and his Church.

It should by now be quite obvious that for John the advent, the crucifixion, the resurrection, and the triumph of Jesus Christ make all the difference in the world. He sees the Old Testament through new eyes, and he so uses it as his source as to emphasise the fundamental truths of Christianity and to present them before our eyes in vivid pictures. With this clue in our hands we should find it possible to interpret much of John's symbolism for ourselves.

We must now turn back to the two passages which we left out, Rev. 13 and 18. They differ from the rest because

John does not seem to interpret them in a particularly Christian sense; that is to say, the fact that the Messiah has come, has been crucified, and has risen again, does not radically alter the significance of the Old Testament passage as it does in the case of the four other passages we have examined:

(3) 13: Many of the details of this chapter come from Daniel (see p. 95). Now in Daniel these symbols have a very definite meaning: the Beast is the Seleucid King Antiochus Epiphanēs, who in 166 B.C. made a determined effort to stamp out Judaism in Palestine and place in its stead the worship of the Greek Pantheon. He even set up a statue of Olympian Zeus in the Temple at Jerusalem. Nebuchadnezzar's image must refer to this incident. What John has done is to transfer this set of symbols (the meaning of which he no doubt understood) and apply them to his day. The historical parallelism is certainly remarkable: the Beast is the Roman Empire with its policy of persecuting Christianity, and the setting up of the image refers to the Emperor-worship which was obligatory on all members of the empire and which the Christians resolutely refused to accept. He is not here using the Old Testament to illustrate specifically Christian beliefs, but nevertheless he is using it in a most significant and effective manner.

(4) 18: John has here taken Ezekiel's prophecy against Tyre and applied it to Rome (Babylon=Rome throughout his book). It is certainly strange that he should choose this prophecy against Tyre to adapt for his 'Babylon', when he had several against Babylon in the Old Testament to choose from (e.g. Isa. 14. 4 ff.); no doubt the fact that Rome was a great commercial sea power determined his choice.[1] Ezekiel's prophecy, it is interesting to observe, did not come true (Ezekiel admits as much, Ezek. 29. 17 f.). Tyre did not fall for about two hundred and fifty years after his prophecy. Similarly, Rome did not fall for three hundred and fourteen years after John's prophecy.

[1] Rome was not a seaport; Ostium was its port at the mouth of the Tiber.

But, just because it was Rome against which John used Ezekiel's material, we feel the sense of anti-climax far less in the case of John's than of Ezekiel's utterance. Rome was then the civilised world; consequently, when we read John's prophecy we can read it quite easily, not as an isolated utterance against a city of the ancient world such as Ezekiel's was, but as an eternal picture of what happens to a civilisation which attempts to oppose God. We can forget Rome of A.D. 96 and see a universal symbol of judgment, as we cannot without a conscious effort in the case of Ezekiel. Once more, John has treated his Old Testament material in such a way as to make something greater and more profound out of it.

Some commentators (e.g. Kiddle) have suggested that John thought the Old Testament was a prediction-book of future history and that he believed that every statement about the future made in the Old Testament must have its literal fulfilment in history at some time or another. Indeed, they have even conjectured that John wrote his book largely in order to show how the prophecies of the Old Testament which had not to date been fulfilled would eventually find their fulfilment. Now our study of John's use of the Old Testament must surely make us unwilling to accept this view. We have seen how he never hesitates to adapt the Old Testament to his own use, how he modifies it to suit his purpose, how he uses it as a quarry from which he draws his materials, not as a rigidly laid-down programme to which all the events in his book must conform. But we give two more examples to show how freely John allowed himself to treat the Old Testament when he so desired. The first is again from Rev. 13; we have seen how the picture of the Beast here is drawn from Dan. 7. Plainly therefore John wishes his readers to assume that the prophecy of the Beast in Dan. 7 is fulfilled in the Roman Empire. But if we read on in Daniel, we find that in ch. 8 he has a vision of a Ram. Now surely, if John had believed that every prophecy in the Old Testament must have its literal fulfilment, he would have felt bound to have gone on to give us an interpretation of the Ram. He could not plead that the prophecy had already been fulfilled in previous history, since the Ram comes after the Beast, and the appearance of the Beast is itself a sign of the end. Similarly, we have seen how in Rev. 18 John has taken materials from Ezek. 26 and 27. The taunt-song which Ezekiel uttered against Tyre John applies to Rome. But in Ezekiel Tyre is compared to a ship, a great merchant galleon which puts to sea loaded with goods of all sorts, and which strikes a rock and sinks in mid-ocean (Ezek. 27. 26 ff.). Once more, if John had believed that this prophecy must have a literal fulfilment he would surely have brought into his book an account of the shipwreck. But there is no trace of it in Rev. 18; he gives a list of Rome's merchandise, and he shows us the merchant princes lamenting her fall, but nowhere does he describe her as a ship, far less account her a wreck.

Old Testament Prophecy and the Christian

But this still leaves unanswered the question: 'What is the relevance of Old Testament prophecy for Christians?' It is unlikely that John thought of the Old Testament as mere prediction, a preview of future history foreseen in a magical fashion by the prophets, and we today can certainly not take that view. But there is a most real and valuable sense in which Old Testament prophecy is still valid today. The Old Testament prophets did not foresee the exact course of future history, but they did glimpse something of the principles according to which God works, and when those principles were later exemplified in history their glimpses were certainly continued, or as we say, fulfilled. Two examples must suffice: an anonymous prophet, writing probably when Israel was in exile in Babylon (586–536 B.C.), whose writings are contained in Isaiah 40 – 55, understood something about the way in which God deals with the sin of man, something which early generations had never guessed. He gives us (Isa. 52. 13 – 53. 12) a picture of a man whom he calls 'the Servant of the Lord'. This man was innocent and righteous, yet he was stricken by a dreadful disease and condemned to death by his fellow-Israelites. The prophet declares that by his voluntary acceptance of suffering and death, all undeserved though they were, this man brought release from sin and forgiveness to the Jews, and indeed perhaps to the rest of the world as well. The New Testament writers, among them, of course, John himself, saw in this Suffering Servant a prophecy of Christ. And they were right: not until someone was found perfectly sinless and perfectly obedient to the will of God could a satisfactory basis be laid for the re-establishment of that fellowship between God and man which sin had broken. And when such a man should appear it was inevitable that the sin of man should put him to death. This much the sixth-century prophet saw, though he did not see Jesus of Nazareth, as literalists would claim. The second example is dealt with at length in the note on chapter 13, p. 95. We have seen how the author of Daniel shows us his vision of the Beast in chapter 7 of his work, a vision which John adapts in Rev. 13. The author of Daniel meant the vision to refer to Antiochus Epiphanēs, John applied it to Rome. But the principle behind both is the same: man is made by God for worship. If he will not worship the true God, then he worships a false one, in one shape or another, and gives it the absolute allegiance which rightly belongs to God alone. This principle was observed in pre-Christian history by the author of Daniel, but it only received its supreme and clearest exemplification when the true God had revealed himself supremely and clearly in Jesus Christ. The connection between Daniel and Revelation is not one whereby a magic prediction magically comes true, but it is one whereby true prophecy has its true fulfilment.

10. John's Literary Technique

The beautiful English of the Authorised Version conceals from us a very remarkable characteristic of John's style, its rough and ungrammatical nature. John must have thought in Hebrew (or Aramaic), and his Greek is stiff and full of the sort of mistakes a foreigner, especially a Semitic-speaking foreigner, would make. This does not mean that it is ineffective; sometimes its very strangeness enhances the effect; nor is it vulgar and uneducated. But his Greek style, like

INTRODUCTION

his material, is unique in the New Testament. Here are a few verses, beginning from 1. 4, translated in such a way as to recall something of what his book must have sounded like to the educated Greek of his day:

'John to the seven churches in Asia: Grace to you and peace from He Is and He Was and He Is to Come, and from the seven spirits they are before the throne, and from Jesus Christ, He the faithful witness, the firstborn of the dead and the ruler of the kings of the earth. To Him that loved us and loosed us from our sins in His blood and He made us a kingdom, priests to God and His Father, to Him the glory and the power for ever and ever. Amen.'

Revelation is a book full of colours and sounds; it has in this respect the attractive simplicity of a child's picture-book, but it has also the cosmic range of *Prometheus Bound* or *King Lear*. John fairly throws colours and sounds at us. Just think of some of his colours. His whites: white robes, a white throne, a white horse, a white stone, a white cloud. His reds: a red horse, a red dragon, a scarlet beast, a woman clothed in purple; and everywhere, in and out of the pictures, blood: a robe dipped in blood, blood up to the bridles, drunk with the blood of the saints. Or his golds: golden harps, golden crowns, the woman holding a golden cup, golden censers, a golden girdle. Or consider the part which fire plays in his pictures: eyes of fire, lamps of fire, fire from heaven, lightning. Then there are his sounds, an astonishing gamut: thunders, trumpets, the sound of many waters, a lion roaring, harps, hail, a multitude singing, an earthquake, a voice from the altar. Add to this those cries that one hears echoing through the book: Alleluia! Fallen, fallen is Babylon the great! Come! Woe! It is done! Notice also John's habit of introducing isolated acts in the middle of an otherwise connected series of events: a star falls from heaven; a millstone is hurled into the sea; an angel flies in mid-heaven; a voice cries, 'A measure of wheat for a penny!' All this has what can only be described as a disconcerting effect on the reader; no doubt it was exactly the effect John would have wished to produce, and that he does produce it reveals the power of his genius. We are shaken out of the pose of disinterested spectator, we are lost in amazement. We begin to feel the awe and wonder which a proper understanding of what is involved in these events would inspire. It is John's method of predisposing our minds to see things in their true perspective.

Another element in John's art which deserves notice is his use of what some psychologists have called 'archetypal images'. There are certain very deep-rooted images which the human mind uses to interpret the outside world to itself, to make sense of its own experiences. Some of these images are found in all mythologies and folk-lores the world over, and when we meet them we probably recognise something familiar about them, though we cannot say exactly what it is since these images are buried deep in our unconscious mind. Mr. C. S. Lewis has drawn attention to them in the works of Milton. The examples which he gives are Heaven, Hell, Paradise, God, Devil, the Winged Warrior, the Naked Bride, the Outer Void.[1] Some of these Miltonic 'archetypal images' listed by Mr. Lewis we can recognise also in Revelation (e.g. Paradise in 2. 7 and 22. 2), but there are a number of others which spring to the mind at once. But before we mention them, it is important to see how John uses them. Mr. Lewis points out that Milton does not attempt to *describe* these images to us; he knows that such a thing would be bound to end in anti-climax and disillusion. Instead he *refers* to them, he touches on them in his narrative in such a way as to get our imagination at work on them, leaving us to do the envisaging for ourselves. John's technique is very similar: he refers to these basic images without explanation: they come into his narrative in the same way as the traditional elements of folk-lore come into a fairy-story, without needing explanation or justification. Here are some of these 'archetypal images'; it is not an exhaustive list: the Old Dragon (12. 9 and 20. 2); the Book of Life; the Key (of David, of the Abyss); the Great Feast at the end of the Hard Won Day (19. 9: compare Lewis

[1] *A Preface to Paradise Lost*, p. 46.

Carroll's use of this in *Alice through the Looking Glass*); the Morning Star (like the Holy Grail, the prize of the victor, 2. 28); War in Heaven; the Sea giving up its Dead; the City of Precious Stones; Gog and Magog gathered to battle; Armageddon. Nearly all these images could be paralleled in Oriental or European folk-lore; some of them are directly traceable to Persian or Babylonian sources. John has in the most skilful manner used these elements, which lie very deep in the unconscious mind even of civilised man, to impress on us some of the fundamental experiences and truths of the Christian faith.

Two more small points are interesting in this connection: the first is what might be called the dream element in John's narrative. We may be quite sure that John is not always using his art consciously; he claims that he is recording visions, and there are a few indications that sometimes his claim is literally true. Consider 'I wept much' in 5. 4; weeping seems a strange reaction to what he saw, and irrational tears are an element in dreams. This may also explain the lack of dimensional proportion in his visions, which has often perplexed the artist trying to illustrate the book, e.g. the two huge angels in 10. 1 and 18. 1, also the impossibility of visualising exactly the relative positions of the various figures in chapters 4 and 5. One might also cite the fantastic size of the locust army in 9. 16: 200,000,000 strong, and the incredible weight of the hailstones in 16. 21: about 120 lb. each. Compare also the way in which voices sometimes break into his narrative without warning. A generation which is getting more and more used to surrealist art (it is now markedly influencing advertisements and even variety technique on the radio) ought to be more at home with John's surprising images and juxtapositions than some of its more matter-of-fact predecessors. The other point is the liturgical character of some of the book; it looks as if John sometimes uses material drawn from the Church's worship, or else material intended for use in worship: 'Holy, holy, holy' (a quotation from Isa. 6, of course); 'Woe, woe, woe'; the refrain 'No more at all in thee' in 18. 21-23 (not found as a refrain in the Old Testament sources for this passage); the antiphonal and liturgical form of many of the songs scattered throughout the book; and the careful selection and juxtaposition of epithets for Christ in the first three chapters, which remind us of the prayers of the historic Christian liturgies.[1]

11. The Devotional Use of Revelation

Many people would be surprised at the idea that Revelation is at all capable of devotional use, but we have already seen that it is a complete mistake to imagine that it is in any sense an 'unchristian' book. It is certainly difficult to use it devotionally without a certain amount of understanding, but in its devotional aspect, as in all others, it yields up its treasures to sympathetic and patient study. There is much of great value in it for Christians who wish to use it as a means of drawing closer to God in meditation and prayer, and it would be a great pity if it were to be ignored because its treasures are not on the surface. Nowhere in the New Testament are we made more vividly conscious of Christ's power and triumph and purity, of the wonderful nature of his victory, and of the thanksgiving and praise which we are impelled to offer to God in response to the divine initiative.

For the ordinary Christian there are three main places in Revelation which are suitable for devotional use: the first of these is the beginnings and endings of each of the letters to the churches in chapters 2 – 3, together with John's vision of Christ in chapter 1 and what precedes it. Every one of the epithets applied to Christ there is worth study and meditation, for each reminds us of some aspect of his nature and work. Similarly, the 'victory' passages at the end of the Letters, beginning 'To him that overcometh' are full of profound and inspiring material for meditation. Secondly, there are the songs scattered throughout the book, with their magnificent attributions of praise to God the

[1] Perhaps the arrangement of the four and twenty elders round about the golden altar which is before God's throne reproduces the early Christian custom whereby the presbyters sat in a semi-circle behind the altar at the Eucharist (cf. Dix, *The Shape of the Liturgy*, p. 28).

Father and to Christ. The third place is in the last two chapters, where we have John's portrayal of eternity. Eternal life, as the other John (the author of the Fourth Gospel) teaches us, begins here, and much that Revelation has to say about 'the new heaven and the new earth' is very relevant to our condition in this life. We will take an example from each of these places in an attempt to give some idea of how they may most profitably be handled.

Chapter 1. 5-6 holds, for such a short passage, an astonishing wealth of material for meditation. Notice how the three epithets for Jesus follow his life, death, resurrection, and ascension: 'the faithful witness', faithful to death as a witness to God's love which he incarnated; 'the firstborn of the dead', and therefore a witness to the triumph as well as to the activity of God's love; 'the prince of the kings of the earth', because he represented God's love, and because that love triumphed. It is a love that cannot ultimately be opposed without disaster. 'Unto him that loved us and washed us' (better R.V. 'loosed us'): by the use of the past tense we are reminded that this was an act of God in Christ, a decisive act in history. 'And hath made us kings (better R.V. 'a kingdom') and priests unto God and his father': here we have a reminder of the church and of the individual Christian's duty of witness—practically the whole creed in two verses!

Turn now to 7. 12: here is the song of the angels to the Father and the Son as they contemplate the martyrs triumphant in heaven. At first glance, it seems just an aggregate of words of praise, heaped together in order to make an effect by sheer quantity. But examine each word separately, and we find that each has its own contribution of meaning to give to the whole. 'Blessing' is that spontaneous act of thanks which men utter when they realise more vividly than ever before their happiness. 'Glory' is the acknowledgement of God's character—his holy, self-giving love as revealed in Jesus. 'Wisdom' is the confession that God has proved wiser than man, in the way he went about man's salvation; it is tantamount to an act of faith in God. 'Thanksgiving' is a more formal act of praise, the Greek is *eucharistia*, and in the minds of John's readers it was not dissociated from the weekly eucharist in which they offered their 'sacrifice of praise and thanksgiving' to God. 'Honour' is the public admission of God's existence and character for which the Church works and to which it looks forward at the end of the ages. 'Power' is the confession of God's ability and right to act as he chooses. 'Might' is the proclamation of God's power as visible in the events of history or super-history.

Finally, look at 21. 3-5: in verse 3 we have a picture of what it will be like when God's plan, revealed in Jesus Christ, is brought to its consummation. But observe that the plan is already fulfilled in principle. God *has* tabernacled with men (John 1. 14); he *has* chosen a peculiar people for himself of which all men may be members. The only difference is that in the perfect state all men will be members of it. In a sense, 'the former things are passed away' already (verse 4), for Jesus Christ has brought a new dispensation, a new relationship between God and man. And when God in verse 5 says 'Behold, I make all things new', John would not have us think of a 'new creation' *after* the 'new creation' of which Paul speaks (2 Cor. 5. 17), but rather of the perfect consummation of that new creation, whereby not only part of the world has accepted the divine rebirth, but all that exists is made new in Christ and the original creation restored and redeemed. It is thus fitting that the Bible should end as it began on a high theme which can be expressed only in mythical and symbolic terms, whilst its centre should be set foursquare in the Incarnation of the Son of God, where eternity expresses itself in time, and myth and history meet. Jesus himself is the key to the scriptures, and in him we can understand the framework of the first and last things in which the Bible sets his ministry.

12. Some Useful Books

There are very few books available on Revelation which are up to date and do not demand a knowledge of Greek. One very good one, about the same size as this, is *The Book of Revelation*, by E. F. Scott (S.C.M. Press), originally published in 1939 and reprinted several times. It is a readable and sound general survey of the book and of the issues it raises, without being a commentary.

Of commentaries, the relevant sections on Revelation in Peake's *Commentary on the Bible* (Nelson) and *A New Commentary on Holy Scripture* (S.P.C.K.) may be consulted, but neither is as full as the present book. More useful is the commentary in the *Century Bible* (T. C. and E. C. Jack) series by Anderson Scott, 1912; it is especially good in its references to the rest of the Bible. It can often be picked up secondhand. Another one is that in the *Moffatt Commentary* series, by Martin Kiddle, assisted by M. K. Ross (Hodder & Stoughton, 1940). This is a big volume of over five hundred pages and inclined to be diffuse. More comparable in its scope is *The Apocalypse of Saint John* by R. J. Loenertz, O.P., a Dominican from Luxembourg (Sheed & Ward, 1947). He divides the book into a septenary of septenaries which, like all clear-cut schemes of division of Revelation, runs into difficulties; but his exegesis is suggestive even though on some major points, e.g. the Millennial City, we are compelled to disagree with him.

Dr. Austin Farrer's large-scale study of Revelation, *A Rebirth of Images* (Dacre Press) appeared when this book was already in type. Time will be needed to sift his conclusions. It presupposes a good knowledge of the contents of of Revelation, of its general background and, indeed, of the Bible as a whole.

COMMENTARY

THE REVELATION OF SAINT JOHN THE DIVINE

The title 'Divine' was given to John, some centuries after he wrote, to call attention to his accomplishments; it is equivalent to saying 'John the Theologian'.

I

THE PROLOGUE
(Ch. 1)

1. 1-3: Solemn Introduction

This takes the place of a title page and preface in a modern book. God has given to Jesus the Messiah a revelation of what he is shortly to accomplish, for him to pass on to his servants. This he does to his servant John by an angel. John in turn passes it on to the churches and solemnly bears witness to what he saw in his visions, namely Jesus Christ's testimony to God's word; and utters a blessing on those who will read aloud his prophecy in the assemblies of the church and lay to heart what he has written. For there is only a short time before the events will happen, and it is necessary that faithful Christians should be warned and ready.

The word translated SERVANT, here as elsewhere in the New Testament is the same as the one for slave; the Christian is at the same time the slave of Christ and God's free man. This angel appears again at the end in 22. 16, and others figure prominently in the book. It is odd that John hears Christ's messages through the help of an angel, and not direct. Angels in this sense of the word developed in later Jewish thought, especially apocalyptic, when God was thought to be unapproachable in his majesty and therefore intermediary spirits were necessary. The Christian faith is that he himself approached man in Jesus Christ. Or it may be, as Loenertz suggests, that this is another instance of John applying to Christ attributes of Yahweh. Jesus sent *his* angel as Yahweh in many O.T. narratives sent his, e.g. Gen. 16. 7. However, John soon makes clear that the risen Christ himself appears to his servants, and there is no doubt throughout that it is Christ's revelation of God's purposes which John sees. For this thought compare many passages in St. John's Gospel, especially 7. 16. The third verse is the first of seven beatitudes, or blessings, which are to be found in the book (14. 13; 16. 15; 19. 9; 20. 6; 22. 7, 14). His conviction that the time is at hand is very like Jesus' own message at the beginning of his ministry 'the time is fulfilled, the kingdom of God is at hand' (Mark 1. 15). The Messiah had already come and won his victory over sin and death, now the victory is to be completed. The lightning of his coming had been seen; now the thunder of his final triumph is to sound.

1. 4-8: Greetings, and the Offering of Praise to the Risen Christ

John's revelation begins with messages to seven churches in the Roman province of Asia before he describes the accomplishment of the Last Things. He wants the church to be the church in reality, not only in name, in the approaching trial, and to this end he scrutinises seven churches (the perfect number) to estimate their spiritual strength for the testing days ahead and to help them correct their faults in time. The judgments passed on the churches of varying degrees of praise and blame are very different, and the churches are undoubtedly meant to stand in their diverse conditions for the Christian Church as a whole. According to Sir William Ramsey (*The Letters to the Seven Churches*), they were selected because they stood on the circular road which bounded the west-central region of the province (see frontispiece). After ch. 4 there is no further contrast between the ideal and the actual church, the contrast is between the faithful and the ungodly.

John utters a threefold greeting: Grace and peace from

HIM WHICH IS, AND WHICH WAS, AND WHICH IS TO COME; AND FROM THE SEVEN SPIRITS WHICH ARE BEFORE HIS THRONE; AND FROM JESUS CHRIST. Grace and peace are great New Testament words which take us back especially to the Epistle to the Romans; the first has no technical meaning, as in later theology, but is simply the graciousness and good pleasure of God which has been shown supremely through Jesus Christ; the second means the harmony between God and man through Jesus Christ, who has removed the alienation which previously existed (cf. Rom. 5. 8 and 2 Cor. 5. 19). They both come in the first place from God; and John like a good Jew refrains from writing his name directly but paraphrases it in the words of God's revelation to Moses in Ex. 3. 14. In the second place grace and peace come from the seven spirits before the throne, who occur again in the vision of heaven (4. 5), and symbolise and personify divine power and perfection (the roots of this idea are to be found in Isa. 11. 2 and Ps. 104. 4, and outside the Bible in Babylonian theories that the sun, moon and five planets are controlled by seven spirits). Finally grace and peace come from Jesus himself. In these few phrases of verse 5 we get echoes of several Bible passages, including Ps. 89. 27; Isa. 55. 4; John 18. 37 and Col. 1. 18; and also a possible dig at the Emperor, who thought himself the source of grace and peace.

There follows the first of the doxologies to Jesus Christ as Saviour and Redeemer, which, as we saw in the Introduction, are so remarkable for a monotheistic Jew; the only other book in the New Testament which has one is 2 Pet. 3. 18, which is the latest to be written. John was overpowered by the Christian conviction of all that God had done through Jesus. The R.V. translation is better: 'that loveth us (all the time) and loosed us (once and for all) from our sins'. Through trust in Christ we are made a kingdom (R.V.), a society the members of which have the priestly privilege of offering spiritual sacrifices of praise and thanksgiving and their own bodies (Rom. 12. 1) in self-surrender. The thought here is akin to that of Heb. 9 and 10. In these phrases the church is put in the centre and linked closely with Christ, a point which is a key feature of the Apocalypse. John offers no worked out *theory*, any more than other New Testament writers do, of how Christ's death avails for the Christian. Even today the church has no defined doctrine of the Atonement. But the whole New Testament is full of the *fact* that the power of sin is overcome in those whose trust is placed in the God of such goodness and love as is seen in the cross of Jesus. It is the worship of such a Saviour that John opposes to that of the Emperor; in the succinct words of F. D. Maurice, 'he opposed the God-man to the man-God' (*op. cit*). Verse 7 is from Dan. 7. 13 (quoted Mark 14. 62) and Zech. 12. 10 (quoted Matt. 24. 30 and John 19. 37—a passage originally referring probably to Simon Maccabeus, a brother of Judas). John reaches this point in his narrative at 19. 11. EVEN SO is the Greek way of saying *Amen*. God himself speaks in verse 8, echoing verse 4. Alpha and Omega are the first and last letters of the Greek alphabet. John changes the customary 'which shall be' to 'which is to come', and reaches this point in his narrative at 20. 11.

1. 9-20: John's account of his command to write the book and his vision of the Risen Christ

John was in prison on the small and rocky island of Patmos, which is off the coast of Asia Minor about fifteen miles from Ephesus, and which, according to the Roman historian Pliny, was used as a penal settlement by the Romans. He was here ON ACCOUNT OF (the best translation) THE WORD OF GOD AND FOR THE TESTIMONY OF JESUS CHRIST. These are the same phrases he used in verse 2; what he is about to set down is in full continuity with the faith he had previously professed. His fondness for threes, of which there have already been examples in this chapter, is seen by his description of the Christian life as tribulation, kingdom and patience, of which he is a fellow-partaker. We get a brief glimpse here of his grasp of Jesus' teaching, who had said 'In the world ye shall have tribulation', and 'It is your father's good pleasure to give you the kingdom', and 'In your patience ye shall win your souls'. There is also an echo of St. Paul; 2 Thess. 3. 5; 2 Cor. 1. 6f. (Note that the R. V. omits the first clause of verse 11.)

REVELATION 1. 9–20

He fell into a trance one Sunday (the first mention of the new weekly Christian resurrection festival in these terms) and, like Peter in Acts 11. 5, heard a voice, one similar to that heard by Ezekiel (Ezek. 3. 12). It was the voice of the Son of Man, the mysterious figure of Dan. 7. 13 and Dan. 10, whose title was taken by Jesus. On the description of him, see the Introduction pp. 35, 37. It is a mistake to try and make these into a coherent portrait as some artists have done. John is describing the indescribable and heaping up phrases from the O.T. and the Book of Enoch to indicate the splendour and authority of the Messiah, a splendour and authority which had hitherto been ascribed only to God. The Father is prior to the Son of Man only in his absolute existence (cf. 1. 4 with 1. 17), as creator (cf. 3. 14 and 4. 11), and as final judge (20. 11). Otherwise the Son is THE FIRST AND THE LAST (cf. verse 8), he is ALIVE FOR EVERMORE and has THE KEYS OF HELL AND OF DEATH (hell is better rendered Hades as in R.V. There is no distinction intended between the words; both mean the abode of the dead waiting the final judgment, which is thought of as having gates, as in Isa. 38. 10).

Yet there is no occasion to fear in spite of the sternness of the Gospel typified by the two-edged sword (Heb. 4. 12); the Messiah is walking in the midst of seven golden candlesticks (Greek—lampstands) which stand for the churches. Here is an echo of the seven-branch candlestick of the tabernacle (Ex. 25. 31) and of a vision of Zechariah (Zech. 4. 2). Moreover, he has conquered death; the best rendering of the end of verse 17 and the beginning of verse 18 is 'I am the first and the last and he that was alive, and died; and I am alive for evermore'. John's fear is like that of Dan. 8. 17, and of the disciples at the Transfiguration (Matt. 17. 6 f.).

With the authority of the crucified and risen Messiah John is commissioned to write (again it is threefold) THE THINGS WHICH THOU HAST SEEN (the vision of this chapter), and THE THINGS WHICH ARE (the letters to the seven churches and the vision of heaven), and THE THINGS WHICH SHALL BE HEREAFTER (all that follows after ch. 5). At the beginning of verse 20 something like 'as for' the mystery . . . must be understood. MYSTERY here as in 17. 7 has the sense of symbol. The angels of the churches here may be 'guardian angels', but more probably, in view of what follows, they are the ideal personification of the churches as contrasted with the actual ones (the candlesticks); and although the Messiah is closely in touch with the actual churches as he moves amongst the candlesticks (verse 13), in their ideal aspect they are at his right hand. On the other hand to John everything has an angel, e.g. the waters (16. 5), fire (14. 18), the abyss (9. 11), in some way in control, and so the angel here may be the leader or leaders of each church. We cannot be sure.

II

THE LETTERS TO THE SEVEN CHURCHES

(Ch. 2 and 3)

JOHN is here addressing seven local churches, but also, as the number indicates, the whole Church as well. Each letter has a similar pattern: (1) a command to write to the angel of the church; (2) the phrase THESE THINGS SAITH followed by a description of Christ, mostly taken from one or other of the details of the vision of the Son of Man in 1. 13-18; (3) the words I KNOW begin an account of the state of the church; (4) there is an exhortation either to continue faithful, or to repent; (5) there is a promise TO HIM THAT OVERCOMETH; (6) there is the solemn sentence beginning HE THAT HATH AN EAR . . . recalling Jesus' own words, addressed each time to churches as a whole. In other details they vary. They all pose the question: In what condition is the church to meet its hour of trial? The *name* of Christian by itself is not enough; there must be the *reality* of love, loyalty and obedience. The letters are an illustration of 1 Pet. 4. 17: judgment begins at the house of God; it will end in Christ's final victory.

2. 1-7: The Letter to the Church in Ephesus

Ephesus was the capital of the Roman province of Asia, the terminus of the east-west trade routes through Asia

Minor—the greatest commercial centre of the country, and the possessor of the famous temple of Diana. Its great strategic importance was probably why St. Paul stayed there longer than at any other place, first preaching in the synagogue for three months, and then for two years in the school or lecture-room of Tyrannus. On all this see Acts 19. It became one of the chief Christian centres of the East Mediterranean and was probably the home both of our John and the author of the fourth gospel. Nothing remains of it today.

The description of verse 1 is taken from 1. 16. Their efforts to labour for Christ, to overcome error and to remain steadfast, recall St. Paul's greeting to the church at Thessalonica (1 Thess. 1. 3). False apostles were a great problem to the early Church, especially people with a Greek background who had little understanding of Hebrew thought and therefore misunderstood fundamental Christian language (see verse 6). The Epistle to the Ephesians (very probably by St. Paul) tells the church there to 'have no fellowship with the unfruitful works of darkness, but rather reprove them' (5. 11), and the first Epistle of John warns its readers to 'believe not every spirit, but try the spirits whether they are of God; because many false prophets are gone out into the world' (4. 1); cf. also Matt. 24. 24. This the Ephesians had done, but, like the Jewish people of old, they were forgetting their love to God (Matt. 24. 12) and were in danger of being disowned and having their candlestick moved. No one knows who the Nicolaitans were or the Balaamites of verse 14, but the general guess is that they were people who carried to extremes the liberty of the Christian man who lives not under law but under grace, and were licentious. St. Paul had repeatedly to defend himself against the charge of being one of them. The early Church had a continual battle with them, for many people, influenced by the popular Greek thought of the time, held that Christianity was a 'spiritual' religion and that material things were therefore of no consequence to it; as a result some became ascetics and some libertines. The nearest equivalent today are those who say Christianity has nothing to do with politics and daily affairs. The opposite of 'spiritual' in the New Testament is not 'material', but 'carnal'.

The reward of those who overcome (which will include martyrdom) is to eat of the tree of life and immortality, which was in the Garden of Eden (Gen. 2. 9) and is to be placed once more in the heavenly Jerusalem when there is a new heaven and a new earth (22. 2, 14). PARADISE is a Persian word for garden; it has now come to mean the heavenly garden of God (Luke 23. 43).

In verse 7 and in the corresponding place in each of the seven letters it is THE SPIRIT who utters a message; in 1. 10 John is IN THE SPIRIT, and in 22. 17 THE SPIRIT AND THE BRIDE SAY, COME. It is probable that in Revelation John always means the prophetic spirit sent by Christ. He is not concerned to make precise distinctions, but holds that the victory of Christ has resulted in the spirit of prophecy being present in the Church, whereby the disclosure of the final purpose of God is made possible and it can be shown how 'the mystery of God should be finished' (10. 7). How John conceived of his prophetic function is indicated by the Book of Revelation itself, and especially by his creative reinterpretation of the Old Testament (Introduction, section 9). In his thought the Spirit of Christ and the Spirit of prophecy can hardly be distinguished, and in 22. 17 it is probably the former which is uppermost in his thoughts.

2. 8-11: The Letter to the Church in Smyrna

Smyrna is about fifty miles north of Ephesus and, being on the coast at the end of another great trade route, it was the commercial rival of Ephesus. It had a large Jewish settlement (verse 9). We do not know how Christianity first came there, unless Acts 19. 10 gives us a clue. One of its early Bishops was Polycarp, who was martyred in 155. It is the only one of the seven cities still in existence.

THE FIRST AND THE LAST comes from 1. 17 (cf. also 1. 8 where it is applied to God); the Messiah also 'was dead and came to life' (Moffatt): R. H. Charles suggests their poverty may have been due to despoiling of their goods by Jewish or pagan mobs; for their riches see Jas. 2. 5. John is in full accord with Paul's claim that the Christians are the true Israel, and a Jew who understood his own faith properly would acknowledge Jesus as the Messiah (cf. Rom. 2. 28). But most Jews were bitterly hostile to Christianity, partly because it seemed blasphemous to worship a Galilean peasant who was put to death as a criminal, partly because Christians were so successful in evangelising 'god-fearers' who hovered on the edge of Judaism, attracted by its monotheism and lofty ethic but unable to accept circumcision and the food laws. Hence John calls them a SYNAGOGUE OF SATAN. Satan, who originally tested men's faith (Job 1 and 2) has now become the personification of evil and identified with the serpent of Gen. 3 (12. 9). The account of the martyrdom of Polycarp shows the savage joy with which Jews helped the Romans to persecute Christians. The Jews alone among Rome's subjects were excused Emperor-worship (on condition he was prayed for in the synagogues), a tribute to their persistence in their religion. But the Christians had no such protection; they were disowned by the Jews and appeared to the Roman authorities to be a troublesome, eccentric, and potentially dangerous sect. Hence John sees them as about to suffer the kind of persecution which has influenced our Gospel narratives (e.g. Luke 21. 12) for TEN DAYS (i.e. a short time) that they MAY BE TRIED (Jas. 1. 12). If they are FAITHFUL UNTO DEATH as Christ was (Phil. 2. 8) they will receive a CROWN OF LIFE. This is the victor's wreath in the games for which Smyrna was famous and which to the Christian is the symbol of eternal life (Paul used the same illustration with reference to the even more famous Corinthian games in 1 Cor. 9. 25), and escape from the SECOND DEATH. The first death is the natural one, the second is the final annihilation and destruction of what is opposed to God which John portrays in 11. 16 and refers to in 20. 6 and 21. 8. There is no death in the new heaven and the new earth.

2. 12-17: The Letter to the Church in Pergamum (A.V., Pergamos)

Pérgamum was still another fifty miles north and fifteen

inland. It had been the capital of a state and was historically of more importance than the previous two cities, but had now lost ground to them. But it was the strongest centre of paganism of the seven places; no wonder John says it is WHERE SATAN'S SEAT IS. It was the centre of the worship of Aesculapius, the god of healing, whose symbol was a serpent—to the Christian the symbol of Satan. Further it was the spiritual Rome of the East, the stronghold of the Imperial Cult, and had had a temple dedicated to 'divine Augustus' and Rome since 29 B.C. Nor was that the end. Behind the city and dominating it was a 1,000-ft. hill covered with heathen temples.

The description in verse 12 is from 1. 16. Nothing is known of Antipas; he appears to have been the first instance there of Christian martyrdom (almost certainly for refusing to take part in Emperor-worship), which John regards as a foretaste of what is to come (13. 15). The Greek word martyr (A.V.) is the same as witness (R.V.). Since Pergamum is the centre of Emperor worship, John is particularly anxious that Christians should keep themselves wholly apart. To buy meat in the open market was to compromise since it would first have been associated with sacrifices at pagan temples. Yet were Christians to run their own butcher's shops? Paul had to advise the Corinthians to avoid immorality, but otherwise not to worry too much except that they should respect the conscience of the scrupulous (1 Cor. 8. 10; 10. 19; cf. also Rom. 14; and for the connection of this with the decree of the council at Jerusalem of Acts 15. 29 commentaries on Acts should be consulted). John may be taking a rigorist line or else not requiring more than abstention from pagan feasts. At any rate laxity, he holds, leads to licence, whether FORNICATION is taken literally or in the sense (common in the Old Testament) of dealing with false gods. This connects in his mind with the laxity of the Nicolaitans and with the sin of Balaam. Balaam hardly has justice done to him by the Bible, which ignores his obedience to God (Num. 22 – 24) and regards him as the archetype of all false and corrupt teaching (e.g. Jude, verse 11). The meaning of Balaam in Hebrew, 'he hath consumed the people', is nearly the same as that of Nikolaos in Greek. Unlike the Ephesians, the Christians at Pergamum had been too tolerant of the lax; if they did not repent they would find the Messiah against them when his coming judgments were abroad in the earth.

The promises in verse 17 are mysterious. The first can only be understood in the light of the Jewish legend preserved in the Apocrypha in 2 Mac. 2. 1 ff. that at the fall of Jerusalem to Babylon in 586 B.C. the prophet Jeremiah had removed the Ark and its contents and hidden them in a cave at Sinai, and that they would be revealed and restored when the Messiah should come. The Jewish Apocalypse of Baruch says of the Messianic Kingdom 'at that time the stores of manna shall descend from above; and they shall eat of it in those years.' So John promises that the conqueror will eat the hidden manna, the true bread from heaven (John 6. 31 ff.) at the Messianic feast. The second promise is more difficult and we do not know what it means: THE WHITE STONE may be the equivalent of superstitious amulets popular in the ancient world or, more probably, it was a kind of pass which would secure admission to the feast, akin to the pebble which was the sign of citizenship and the right to vote. But what is the NEW NAME WRITTEN, WHICH NO MAN KNOWETH SAVE HE THAT RECEIVETH IT? It may be the new name of the Christian in the heavenly city when all things are made new (21. 5), or it may be the name of Jesus (3. 12; 19. 13), knowledge of which, according to ancient belief about the gods, would enable his followers to share his power. The first alternative seems the more probable. The two promises together signify the blessings and powers offered in the eternal kingdom to the Christian who is faithful unto death.

2. 18-29: The Letter to the Church in Thyatira

Thyătíra was a city of no great importance on the road from Pergamum via Sardis to Laodicea. It had a flourishing dyeing industry; one of its representatives, Lydia, was converted by St. Paul at Philippi (Acts 16. 14 f.).

The description of verse 18 is from 1. 14 f., but the title

SON OF GOD does not occur there. Kiddle suggests that John has deliberately added it here because Apollo, the son of Zeus, was the special god of Thyatira. Biblically, it recalls especially Peter's confession at Caesarea Philippi (Matt. 16. 16) and Ps. 2. 7 (verse 9 of Ps. 2 is quoted in verse 27); it was interpreted by the Jews as Messianic and the early Church had no hesitation in transferring it bodily to the risen Christ. In verse 19 there is the characteristic Christian word CHARITY (love, R.V.), *agape*, a word which was used by the early Church to express a wholly new quality, one which is not very frequent in the Apocalypse. Unlike the Ephesians, the last works of the Thyatirans are more than their first, but like the Christians at Pergamum they are troubled by a lax party in the church. Whether Jezebel is an individual person we cannot tell, but she stands for one or more who, as Jezebel of old seduced Ahab from the true worship of God, encouraged disloyalty among Christians. Probably the question was whether to join in the common meals of the Thyatiran trade guilds, which would be prefaced by a dedication or grace to a pagan deity and which frequently ended in licence. It was, however, difficult to do business at all if one abstained. John in reply (verse 24) says he is not adding any fresh burdens beyond that of the Council of Jerusalem (Acts 15. 28). He had warned them previously (verse 21) and now punishment was coming, and one that would 'fit the crime' (the BED would be one of sickness, verse 22) from the Messiah who SEARCHETH THE REINS AND THE HEARTS; reins is the equivalent of the kidneys, which to a Jew was the seat of the emotions, as the heart was of the thoughts. (Jer. 11. 20). John scornfully refers to those who think that Christian freedom means that they are free to explore the DEPTHS OF SATAN (R.V. deep things) in a broad-minded fashion, a mischievous echo of 1 Cor. 2. 10.

The conquerors are to share in Christ's Messianic rule (verse 26 f. quoting Ps. 2. 8 f.) and to be given THE MORNING STAR who is Christ himself (22. 16); that is to say, in the later imagery of ch. 19. 7, they will be married to the Lamb.

3. 1-6: The Letter to the Church in Sardis

Sardis was about thirty-five miles south of Thyatira on the road to Laodicea; formerly the capital of the kingdom of Lydia, it had sunk under Roman domination to a second-rate town, and an earthquake in A.D. 17 had accelerated the process. Its inhabitants were noted for luxury and licentiousness. John does not hint at any danger of persecution or the presence of intellectual errors as with previous churches, but his condemnation of it is the severest of the lot; the majority in this case have been corrupted, not by danger or by error, but by ease. They had become too much conformed to this world.

The allusion in verse 1 is to 1. 4 and 16. Unlike Paul's description of a Christian 'as dying and behold we live' (2 Cor. 6. 9), they are apparently vigorous, but in fact dead; they have A NAME but they are only nominally Christian. John repeats our Lord's warning to WATCH in words which call to mind Matt. 24. 42 f. They are not quite dead; there are a few who have not garments so dirty that they are unfit for worship; they SHALL BE CLOTHED IN WHITE RAIMENT (Matt. 13. 43) at the marriage of the Lamb (19. 8).

THE BOOK OF LIFE plays a big role in the subsequent judgments (13. 8; 17. 8; 20. 12, 15 and 21. 27). It goes back to the register of the inhabitants of Jerusalem (Isa. 4. 3); then it develops into God's list of his people (Ex. 32. 32), and occurs frequently in apocalyptic literature. In Revelation it means the register of heavenly citizens. Other New Testament references are Luke 10. 20; Phil. 3. 20. The last part of verse 5 echoes Matt. 10. 32.

3. 7-13: The Letter to the Church in Philadelphia

Philadelphia was about thirty miles south-east of Sardis, another small but rich city and an entrepôt town. Like Smyrna, it is approved by John.

There is no reference to ch. 1 this time; HOLY AND TRUE (genuine) are further examples of attributes of God applied to the risen Messiah (6. 10). THE KEY OF DAVID goes back to Isa. 22. 22, where such a key is given to Eliakim; so Christ will omit or exclude from the new Jerusalem, just as he has the keys of hell or Hades (1. 18). The OPEN DOOR in other parts of the New Testament refers to the opportunity for evangelism (e.g. 1 Cor. 16. 9), but here it has the same sense as the previous verse and harks back to the thought found in the book of Isaiah that the gates of Jerusalem will be open for the upright (Isa. 26. 2); so will the gates of the *new* Jerusalem. The same book repeatedly suggests that pagan peoples would be brought to acknowledge the god of the Jews as their god, and verse 9, which echoes the thought of such passages as Isa. 45. 14 and 60. 14, turns the tables on this by saying that the SYNAGOGUE OF SATAN (see 2. 9) would be humiliated into recognising that God has loved the Christians. There is no suggestion that they will be converted, no agony over their fate such as Paul shows as he wrestles with the problem of the rejection of the Jews in Rom. 9 – 11. Nevertheless with supreme confidence John claims these small struggling churches who have only A LITTLE STRENGTH (verse 8) as the true Israel whose destiny is assured even though THE HOUR OF TEMPTATION (R.V. trial) is about to come. Could we say the same today of the Church in e.g. the Far East, where there may be only from two to six Christians to every thousand inhabitants?

The promises to the conqueror in verse 12 are: first, that he will be A PILLAR IN THE TEMPLE OF MY GOD, which must be taken metaphorically, as there is no temple in the heavenly city (21. 22); and, second, that he will have as victor three names written on his forehead (14. 1; 22. 4, and see Isa. 56. 5, R.V.), 'the name of God, for whose pleasure he was created; the name of the new society of the redeemed, to which he eternally belongs; and the name of Christ, in that revelation of himself in glory which is necessarily concealed from those who dwell in this world' (Anderson Scott, *op. cit.*).

3. 14-22: The Letter to the Church in Laodicea

Lā-ō-dĭ-cé-a was south-east of Philadelphia and east of Ephesus, in the Lycus valley, and only a few miles from Colossae, whence Epaphras had come to evangelise it (Col. 1. 7; 4. 12). Paul's letter to it (Col. 4. 16) has been lost. It had rapidly expanded during Roman dominance and became rich (verse 17) as a banking centre and because of its fine quality black wool and woollen goods.

The description of Christ in verse 14 is taken from Isa. 65. 16 R.V. Margin, where AMEN is applied to God; from 1. 5 THE FAITHFUL AND TRUE WITNESS; and from Col. 1. 15 THE BEGINNING OF THE CREATION OF GOD. John may be deliberately alluding here to the epistle to nearby Colossae. No phrase could show more fully his exaltation of Christ, for he is the mediator both of creation and of the *new* creation, THE FIRST-BEGOTTEN OF THE DEAD (1. 5). As the beginning of the *new* creation of God, Christ is the Proper Man; in him we see what man is meant to be.

The spiritual state of Laodicea has become a by-word. Moreover they were completely blind to it and thought they were rich when they of all people (the THOU of verse 17 is very emphatic) were WRETCHED AND POOR. I COUNSEL THEE TO BUY goes back to Isa. 55. 1 ff. and the OF ME is emphatic. They were to buy GOLD TRIED (R.V. refined) IN THE FIRE, a true and not a counterfeit religion, obtainable not by money but by humility and faith; they should buy the white robes of the Lamb's marriage feast rather than trust in their own black woollens (Matt. 22. 11-14), and eyesalve to remedy their spiritual blindness rather than rely on the special ointment prescribed by the well-known medical faculty at Laodicea. Let them show zeal rather than lukewarmness, and remember that the chastening they can expect is from a Lord who loves them (*philein*, an emotional verb, is used). This thought is found in Prov. 3. 12 and Heb. 12. 6 and again is transferred here from Yahweh to Christ.

The final three verses seem to look almost explicitly beyond the church in Laodicea to the whole Church. Verse 20 calls to mind many echoes of the fourth Gospel, notably 14. 23, but they are too many to quote. There is surely a reference here to the weekly Christian eucharist with Christ as the bread of life, as well as to the great Messianic feast when to HIM THAT OVERCOMETH will be given a place with Christ on his throne and a share in his authority (cf. John 17. 24). With the assurance of Christ's care, with its inmost being responding to the joys of the consummated Messianic kingdom, and nerved by the victory by which he overcame death and sin, the church may be ready to face the coming trial. Finally, let us note that there is no question of separate denominations as in our day: there is one church in Philadelphia and the other cities; all the Christians there are simply the 'church in Philadelphia'.

III

THE VISION OF HEAVEN

(Ch. 4 and 5)

JOHN is pursuing his threefold task of 1. 19. In ch. 1 he describes what he had seen, and in ch. 2 – 5 he is dealing with THE THINGS WHICH ARE. The letters to the churches tell of those which are on earth, and now he comes to those which are in heaven. Then from ch. 6 he is ready to detail THOSE WHICH SHALL BE HEREAFTER. Ch. 4 and 5 are complementary and hang upon three great doxologies, the first to God as creator in 4. 11, the second to the Lamb as Redeemer in 5. 9 and 12, and the third to HIM THAT SITTETH UPON THE THRONE AND UNTO THE LAMB in 5. 13; in this last, the whole created world joins as well as heaven and its inhabitants. The Redeemer does not appear in the first vision, which might be said to be the heaven of the old dispensation, and no one dare undertake to execute the divine decrees which have been inscribed in a seven-sealed book. John is downcast because it appears as though evil will continue triumphant and the accomplishment of God's purposes will be delayed, until he sees the Lamb who through his sacrificial death has been found worthy to open the book and carry out God's will in the world (5. 2-5). No angel could open it, only one whose power was made perfect in weakness and who knew earth's conflicts through personal participation in them.

The total effect of John's vision is awe-inspiring in the extreme; mysterious colours, shapes and images heighten the atmosphere of wonder and grandeur, and his aim to concentrate attention on the supreme achievement of Christ and his centrality in the divine purposes is abundantly achieved. When we examine the images more closely we see that they are nearly all traditional, from the Bible and especially from Ezekiel, Isaiah, and Daniel; and behind the Old Testament there lies much Babylonian mythology and astrology. Of the origin of the last he was almost certainly unaware and it is even doubtful if he is even consciously quoting from the Bible, for his mind is steeped in its images, and he never quotes a whole text *verbatim*. From whatever source they come, they are inextricably entangled in these chapters, and it is a mistake to press the details too closely and try to construct a precise visual impression of what he is describing. It is impossible to do so. Mortal man cannot describe heaven; the best he can do is to pile up visual metaphors from the language of the earth. This John has done supremely well because his mind has been formed mainly by the Old Testament, which he regarded as authoritative for the Christian, and which in fact shows by far the most profound understanding of life to be found in the pre-Christian world. On the whole question of John's use of the Old Testament see section 9 of the Introduction.

4. 1-11: Vision of God as Creator

AFTER THIS in verse 1 recurs at 7. 1, 9; 15. 5; 18. 1, and 19. 1, to mark off sections of the narrative. The DOOR OPENED IN HEAVEN recalls 3. 8; the fact that John probably thought of it, in accordance with the ancient picture of the universe, as the door through the ceiling of the sky does not affect the symbolism. FIRST might better be translated 'former', for the voice is clearly that of the Son of Man of 1. 10. Before he can deal with the THINGS WHICH MUST BE HEREAFTER (ch. 6 onwards) he has to describe what now is, as a result of the Lamb's death and victory. The ecstatic state of 1. 10 is renewed.

John sees a THRONE set in heaven AND ONE SAT ON THE THRONE, and refrains even from mentioning the august name. The heaven itself is God's throne, according to Isa. 66. 1 and we must regard this as a symbol of divine power not as a piece of furniture (cf. 16. 17). It is noteworthy that there is no temple in this particular vision of heaven; John sometimes uses 'throne' and sometimes 'temple' as a symbol of God's presence. Kiddle points out that 'temple' is used when John is speaking of God's relation to a rebellious world, and many of the punitive strokes come out of it (11. 19; 14. 15-20; 15. 6-8; 16. 17-18). In trying to describe God, John, like Old Testament writers, can write of no form, but takes refuge in light of all kinds, of a rainbow and of bright and precious stones; this vision recalls the weird imagery of Ezek. 1. and Dan. 7 and the rainbow in Gen. 9.

The FOUR AND TWENTY ELDERS (Greek presbyters) have given rise to immense speculations. Are they angels? Or the twelve tribes (or patriarchs) and twelve apostles? Or the twenty-four courses of priests of 1 Chron. 24? Or Babylonian astral divinities? Most probably they are a kind of 'court' of angels whose presence in heaven was part of Jewish apocalyptic tradition, based on Isa. 24. 23 (R.V. Margin). It is worth while noticing the part they play in the worship of God and the Lamb. One of their number also speaks to John in 5. 5 and 7. 13. LIGHTNINGS AND THUNDERINGS AND VOICES occur later (in 8. 5; 11. 19; 16. 18), and are connected with God's presence in Ex. 19. 16. THE SEVEN SPIRITS OF GOD recall 1. 4 (see note there) and go back to the vision of Zech. 4. 2; THE LAMPS OF FIRE in this verse become the SEVEN EYES of the Lamb in 5. 6. John adapts this one prophecy to illustrate two related themes, God's activity (fire) and his omniscience (eyes). THE SEA OF GLASS LIKE UNTO CRYSTAL figures frequently in apocalyptic thought and goes far back in the Bible. In Gen. 1. 7 the waters that were above the firmament are distinguished from those below it, and the molten sea of Solomon's temple (1 Kings 7. 23) was probably meant to symbolise this heavenly sea, which in turn signifies the distance between God and his creatures even in heaven.[1]

Next we come to the oddest feature of the vision of heaven, THE FOUR BEASTS (a most unfortunate translation of the A.V.; literally it is 'living things'; the R.V. has 'living creatures'). Ultimately they go back to signs of the zodiac— the bull, lion, archer, and eagle—but immediately they are connected with the creatures in the extraordinary vision of Ezek. 1, which we can tell from Ezek. 10. 20 are the cherubim. These are frequently referred to in the O.T. in connection with divine power (Ps. 80. 1; 99. 1, etc.), and there was a representation of them in Solomon's temple (1 Kings 6. 23 ff.). It is hard to say what exactly they meant to the Jews, but they appear to be God's agents, representing his power over all the created world; they are FULL OF EYES BEFORE AND BEHIND (verse 6) AND WITHIN (verse 8) signifying God's omniscience. They also have SIX WINGS, and these they have acquired from the seraphim, the curious winged serpents which Isaiah saw in the temple of Jerusalem (Isa. 6). Their praise of God is found in the same chapter of Isaiah. These living creatures play a considerable part in transmitting God's judgment on the created world (6. 1; 15. 7).[2]

When the living creatures utter their praise, the elders add their hymn to the creator; FOR THY PLEASURE (because of thy will, R.V.) THEY ARE, AND WERE CREATED. Not only has God created all things and persons, but they depend every moment for their continued existence on his will.

Note on John's use of Angels

Angels play a very large part in his book. The two functions which they perform can be distinguished: they carry out God's commands, and they lead the worship which is

[1] The difficulty of interpreting some of John's symbolism is illustrated by A. W. Burnet's *The Lord Reigneth*, p. 61, where he refers to 'the quiet of a calm and glassy sea' and takes it to signify serenity. The Biblical background is usually our chief clue. In this case we doubt whether it suggests serenity.

[2] The traditional association of them with the four evangelists— Matthew as the man, Mark as the lion, Luke as the ox, and John as the eagle—is without foundation.

eternally offered to God in heaven. All the writers of the New Testament apparently accepted the existence of angels as part of their Jewish inheritance. It is difficult to see that it can matter very much today whether we are particularly concerned with the ministerial function of angels or not. Belief in angels originated among the Jews at a time when they were becoming increasingly conscious of the majesty and remoteness of God, and the existence of angels was welcomed as a link between the transcendent God and humble men. But Christians believe that God has himself bridged that gap in Jesus Christ and now offers full and free communion with himself in the Church. Consequently our interest in the ministerial function of angels will probably depend on the extent to which we feel ourselves obliged to accept every circumstance of the New Testament revelation.

The other function which angels fulfil in the Apocalypse, however, that of worship, seems more nearly related to what is essential in the Christian message. When we realise the glory, holiness, and majesty of the Triune God, we can see how appropriate to such a God is the worship of his creatures. God has made all things to his glory (to show forth his nature by being most true to their own nature which he gave them), and the natural response of all created things to him is worship:

'All the earth doth worship thee; the Father everlasting. To thee all angels cry aloud; the Heavens and all the Powers therein.'

It seems most fitting therefore that in the eternal sphere there should be eternal worship offered to God. We cannot understand how it is offered, nor the nature of the beings who lead it. But that there should be this eternal worship, the ideal towards which man's worship on earth aspires, we feel to be most fitting. Note that the angelic worship as conceived by John is joined with the Church's worship. The angels, though they do not share in human nature, join in the worship of the Lamb that was slain for men. We can, then, know very little about the nature or activities of the angelic order, and dogmatism on this subject is merely ridiculous, but we can see why it is that Christian thought has been led to connect them with the worship of heaven, and thus far sympathise with John's frequent reference to them in his book.

5. 1-14: Vision of Christ in Heaven as Redeemer

Ezekiel's book which he was commanded to eat (Ezek. 2. 9 ff.) lies behind the one John saw, and we can imagine it to be made up of leaves of parchment sealed together. It contains the full details of God's fixed purpose for the world. 'Who hath known the mind of the Lord?' asks St. Paul in Romans 11. 34 (quoting Isaiah), as he contemplates the work of God through Christ; and now only the Lamb is worthy to learn the mind of God and to play the decisive part in bringing his plan to fruition. Jesus did not change the divine plan; he unfolded its eternal and unchangeable nature by his obedience even to the death on the cross (Phil. 2. 5 ff.), and at the same time accomplished a decisive stage in it through the creation of the new community, the true Israel. In virtue of this he is to accomplish the final stages through his perfect obedience to the loving and righteous will of God. The unity of the will of the Father and the Son is particularly brought out, but in different language, in the Fourth Gospel and the Epistle to the Hebrews.

With verse 2 compare Isa. 6. 8. Verses 5 and 6 bring us to two of the most profound verses in the whole of the Apocalypse; they relate Jewish Messianic hopes to the distinctively Christian good news of the advent of the Messiah in the person of Jesus of Nazareth, but a Messiah of a character so wholly unexpected by the Jews that they rejected him. This element of the unexpected is brought out with great force by the transition from the LION of verse 5 to the LAMB of verse 6. The Lion goes back to the blessing of his sons by Jacob in Gen. 49. 9, where Judah is described as a 'lion's whelp; from the prey, my son, thou art gone up', a passage which the rabbis interpreted as a prophecy of the Messiah. But the Lion is also the ROOT OF DAVID (see 22. 16); the source of this phrase is an avowedly Messianic prophecy in Isa. 11. 1 ff. which looked to an ideal king of David's line who would combine power and goodness. 'And there shall come forth a rod out of the stem of Jesse and a branch shall grow out of his roots'; upon him would the sevenfold spirit of the Lord rest (verse 6). Yes, says John, the Messiah has come, but as A LAMB AS IT HAD BEEN SLAIN with HORNS signifying power (e.g. Ps. 112. 9) and EYES signifying insight; SEVEN of each signifying completeness. The horns also take us back to Dan. 7. 7, 20, and the eyes to Zech. 4. 10; the eyes, which there belong to God, are attributed by John to Christ. (The Beast in 13. 1 ff. is a blasphemous counterpart of the Lamb.) But by far the most important reference behind the idea of the Lamb is Isa. 53, especially verse 7: 'He is brought as a lamb to the slaughter.' The early Church with one accord saw in this whole passage a foreshadowing of the Messiah who in humility would not *bring* woes on others, as contemporary Jewish thought expected, but *bear* them for others. The word 'Lamb' has become for John almost a proper name. Little of the gentleness of Jesus is left in his thought (but note 7. 17). Yet to John the voluntary sacrifice by Jesus of his life was the key to the whole divine plan; he had died when the Passover lambs were being slain and he is now standing victorious. When John seems to be wholly occupied with the wrath of the Lamb we must never forget that what he means by wrath is governed by a love which gave itself for sinful mankind even to death (see 6. 16).

The elders and living creatures we learn from verse 8 have harps (14. 2) and GOLDEN VIALS FULL OF ODOURS (bowls full of incense, R.V.) WHICH ARE THE PRAYERS OF SAINTS (Ps. 141. 2). This is John's first hint of the participation of the worship of the church on earth in that of the church in heaven, of which more is said in 8. 3 ff. SAINT, of course, is the N.T. name for every Christian (e.g. Rom. 1. 7). They sing a NEW song for Christ has inaugurated a new era. Demands for a new song to celebrate some mighty act of God are found in the O.T., e.g. after the return from exile (Isa. 42. 10; Ps. 96. 1). Christ has REDEEMED US to God (better R.V. purchased, and 'us' omitted) by his blood, and out of all nations, not the Jewish only. PURCHASED

reminds us of 1 Cor. 7. 23. The redeemed are to be KINGS
AND PRIESTS and to REIGN ON THE EARTH. The thought of
1. 6 is repeated with its connection with 1 Pet. 2. 9, cf. Ex.
19. 6, while John looks forward to the millennium, or reign
of Christ with the martyrs for a thousand years, which he
does not reach until ch. 20. Already Christians enjoy two of
these privileges; those struggling churches we read of in
ch. 2 and 3 are already priests in God's kingdom and
exercising the powers of the 'age to come'. We must not
think that John postpones everything to the future.

Further angels join in the first of John's two glorious
concluding doxologies, making a chorus of myriads (Dan.
7. 10) offering a sevenfold worship (notice the number seven
again) to THE LAMB THAT WAS SLAIN. (This is the parallel of
'hast created' in 4. 11.) And now the whole creation, the
entire universe and the whole of heaven itself, joins in an
outburst of praise UNTO HIM THAT SITTETH UPON THE THRONE
AND UNTO THE LAMB, and the living creatures say the solemn
AMEN which John repeats at the end of his book (22. 20).
(Note that the R.V. misses out the last seven words of
verse 14.) Nowhere else in the New Testament is Christ
adored in complete equality with God the creator; the
audacity of it for a Jew makes us realise the impression Jesus
had left on his disciples and the nature of their fellowship
with him after his resurrection.

IV

THREE SERIES OF JUDGMENTS

(Ch. 6 – 16)

We now enter what is certainly the most obscure part of the book, chapters 6 – 16, in which three sets of divine judgments are described, with four parentheses or diversions inserted; the scheme of these chapters is laid out on p. 22, a scheme which is followed in the section headings below. The first set of judgments is the Seven Seals, ch. 6: (4 (*a*) in the scheme on p. 22).

(*a*)

6: The Seven Seals: a Theology of Power

One of the features that distinguishes Revelation from all other books in the New Testament is the fact that its author is attempting what no other New Testament writer attempts on anything like the same scale: to explain to us how *power* fits into the divine scheme of things. (Perhaps today, when mankind has discovered vast new powers without accepting any clear principle according to which they should be used, Revelation is especially relevant.) John begins from the belief that all power comes from God. God is absolute ruler of the world. But when God gave man free will (it is what made him man), he had to allow the posssibility that man might misuse the power thereby entrusted to him, and this possibility was realised. In the world of John's day it seemed that a greater amount of physical power than ever before was being wielded by the most evil hands the world had yet seen. Rome ruled the civilised earth. This did not mean, however, that God was helpless, frustrated by his own gift of power to man. The world was still God's and was still ruled according to his eternal laws of right and wrong. The way God's power was shown in the world was that the misuse of power entailed suffering and disaster. Wars, starvation, devastation, these were the means whereby it was made plain that power abused was still under God's control. These were the 'judgments' of God, the working out on the plane of history of his inexorable moral laws.

Bearing this in mind, one can approach more sympathetically this chapter with its apparently ruthless depiction of suffering and death and its unhesitating attributions of these to God. Notice in verse 4 that a sword is GIVEN to the man on the red horse, as a crown, symbol of victory, is GIVEN to the horseman in verse 2. These, the celebrated 'Four Horsemen of the Apocalypse', come from Zech. 6. 1-8. All these happenings, John would have us understand, are the results of the working out of God's righteous laws for his universe. Things have not got out of control. God does not approve of death and hell and famine, but they are what must follow if men persist in opposing God's rule, and hence they are part of God's purpose. We may legitimately regard the events described in verses 1-8 as brilliant little vignettes of God's judgments working out in history: *this* is what happens in the sphere of politics when men oppose God; and *this* in the military sphere (the events of the year A.D. 69 give colour here; see p. 26); and *this* in the sphere of economics. Similarly the cry of the martyrs in verse 10, so offensive to our ears at first, is only seen in true perspective when we bear in mind John's beliefs about the source of power. Perhaps there is in it a hint of a less than Christian gesire for vengeance, but behind it lies something much deeper, a Christian interpretation of history. God's vendeance is seen when the results of our sins are carried to their disastrous conclusions in human life. The martyrs ask how long it will be before the savage policy of persecution which the Roman Empire had adopted towards the Christian Church will bring its inevitable retribution in failure and shame. Because we live centuries later we know the answer. In A.D. 313 the Emperor Constantine officially ended the state's opposition to Christianity and confessed tne utter failure of the anti-Christian policy.

One of the commentators has pointed out the correspondence between the woes described in the first six seals (ch. 6) and the woes foretold in the thirteenth chapter of St. Mark's Gospel. As we saw in the Introduction (p. 44), the Jews used many images to express what they expected to happen when the Messiah would at last come to his people. The early Church certainly, and probably Jesus himself, took over these images and used them to express the universal significance of the coming of God among man.

In verse 6 the citing of the price of wheat and barley and the command about the oil and the wine appear to mean that there will be a famine, but only a partial one. The penny, or denarius, was a day's wage. The measure (coenix) was just enough to keep body and soul together. The ancient world, as well as the modern, had its difficulties concerning food distribution and price control, and the commentator who points out the contrast here between the care exercised by men over *things* and their reckless expenditure of *persons* is surely not embroidering on the meaning of the passage. If, as has been suggested, we take the first four seals at least as vignettes, or typical scenes of God's judgment in history, verse 8 gives us a very fitting climax to the first three seals. In them we have seen what happens when men ignore the divine laws which govern the world. Now power is given to death and hell (that is to say, the glorification of sheer destruction almost for its own sake), and mere nihilism, the denial of any source of moral standard whatever, is the logical result of the denial of any superhuman authority in the world. Europe after the second world war seems to bear this out.

In verse 9 it is really waste of time to ask 'What altar?' John does not give us a guide book to heaven, and the altar here is mainly significant as a symbol of sacrifice. John connected the sacrifice of the martyrs very closely with the sacrifice of Christ. As Christ offered himself on behalf of all men as the one man who completely fulfilled God's requirements of holiness and obedience to his will, so the Christian martyrs, as members of Christ's body, the church, take their part in that sacrifice, reproducing in their particular moment of history what has been done for all eternity by Christ (cf. Phil. 1. 29; Rom. 12. 1). It is only fair to bear this in mind when we come across a passage in Revelation where God is described as overcoming his enemies in an apparently ruthless fashion. For John, God's way of conquest is first and foremost shown us in Christ's sacrifice on the cross.

In verse 11, R. H. Charles maintains that the WHITE ROBES so often associated with the glorified martyrs in Revelation mean their resurrection bodies. There is a good deal of evidence that in Jewish circles (apocalypses like 1 Enoch and the Ascension of Isaiah) and Christian ones (Matt. 13. 43; Phil. 3. 21), the resurrection body was conceived as a body of light or a body of glory. The thought probably goes back to Ps. 104. 2. If this is so, it shows that John did not believe in the resurrection of the physical body, but agreed with Paul's doctrine of a 'spiritual' body (1 Cor. 15. 43, 49, 54; 2 Cor. 5. 1-4). The possession of the heavenly body, however, is related to earthly conduct; there is a danger we may be found naked (2 Cor. 5. 3), and so it can be said of the faithful martyrs in the next chapter that they are 'arrayed in white robes' which they 'have washed' and 'made them white in the blood of the Lamb' (see 7. 13 f.). In verse 13 THE STARS OF HEAVEN represent (indeed in the N.T. they are sometimes called) the powers of heaven, i.e. those who wield power, whether in the spiritual or material world. The symbolism goes far back into Babylonian mythology in which the stars were accounted gods and believed to influence the world. John was not, of course, consciously borrowing from this source. Compare W. B. Yeats:

> Things fall apart; the centre cannot hold;
> Mere anarchy is loosed upon the world. . . .
> *(The Second Coming)*

HIDE US FROM THE FACE OF HIM THAT SITTETH UPON THE THRONE AND FROM THE WRATH OF THE LAMB (verse 16). The wrath of the Lamb! Can this apply to him who said: 'Father, forgive them, for they know not what they do'? The answer is yes, but only if we realise what John means by 'the wrath of the Lamb'. He has been describing in this chapter what happens when men oppose God's government of the world: chaos, death, disaster—these are the results which must, by the very nature of things, follow from man's sin when it takes its course in the world. But John had something more to say about God than this: God has now in Jesus Christ revealed his nature and his design for men. Something of the very essence of that plan whereby God governs the world has been shown: he has revealed himself as active, self-giving, sacrificial love (that is why the title 'the Lamb' which is applied to Jesus so frequently by John is so significant). Hence rebellion against God is rebellion against divine sacrificial love, and the consequences of that rebellion, inevitably working out in history, are the direct results of the rejection of that love revealed in Christ. This is what John calls 'the wrath of the Lamb'. It is a paradox, and no doubt John never means it to be anything else, but, if we accept his assumptions, we must admit some sort of idea corresponding to 'the wrath of the Lamb'. If sin brings evil consequences (as it must in any morally ordered world), and if God's nature is finally revealed in Jesus Christ, then those who sin are sinning against Jesus, and the world is suffering the consequences of sinning against Jesus. In verse 16, horrified at the results of their own actions, men seek to escape from God. Men still try to escape from God in various ways; compare the behaviour of those people who, horrified at the realities of the atomic era, try to find solace and escape in art and music.

7: *First Parenthesis: the Marking of the Saints and the ultimate triumph of the Redeemed*

The sixth seal has been opened, and, before the opening of the seventh seal, John inserts a scene of a different character. We can only guess why John arranged his material as he did, and there is a risk of attributing too much significance to the particular order in which he presents his visions. It seems very likely that what John has in fact done in this chapter is to adapt for his own purposes two already existing brief prophecies which were current. Verses 1-3 describe the holding of the winds, a piece of imagery which can be paralleled in contemporary Jewish literature. John uses it to enhance the solemnity and significance of the sealing which follows. Verses 4-8 describe the sealing of the twelve tribes of Israel, and the passage may, when John found it, have been meant to refer only to the Jewish nation, or only to the Jews who had joined the Christian Church. The purpose for which John uses it is considered below. Verses 9-17 are John's own composition. Probably John used this particular material at this particular point because he wanted to cheer his readers by a glimpse of the victory of God's servants in the midst of the judgments and destruction which he must record.

The significance of the sealing is not very obvious. It is bound up with the fact that 144,000 are sealed: 12,000 for each of the tribes of Israel. In the source from which John took this fragment the 144,000 no doubt meant all the Jews, or all the faithful Jews; but for John, as for all the N.T. writers, Israel cannot be limited to Jews by race alone. The *new* Israel is the Christian Church; it is indeed only Christians who now have the right to call themselves Jews, God's chosen people (see 3. 9 and note). Hence when John writes in verse 4: I HEARD THE NUMBER OF THEM WHICH WERE SEALED . . . OF ALL THE TRIBES OF THE CHILDREN OF ISRAEL, he must be telling us something about the Christian Church. What is more, the number 144,000 indicates completeness: twelve was the full number of the tribes of God's people; twelve times twelve means the full number of individuals; multiplied by 1,000 it signifies the vastness of the Church in heaven (cf. 21. 17). The Church then, in some sense the complete Church, is being sealed. Now 'sealing' is an image used more than once in the Bible. In John 6. 27 Jesus is described as sealed by God. In 2 Cor. 1. 22, Paul says that God sealed us and gave us his spirit. In Rom. 4. 11, circumcision is described as the seal of faith. All these uses of the word have the sense of setting apart, marking as different from the rest of the world, dedicating. As we shall see later on, the devil has his own parody of this sealing (13. 16). Putting all this together, we may safely conclude that we have in this scene a picture of all the Christians who will remain faithful during the coming trial when the Beast appears. Their being sealed now is an indication that they will remain faithful throughout all the persecutions yet to come. It is a picture of the faithful Church, composed of those who were dying as John wrote, and who would die in the future.

In verse 9 THE GREAT MULTITUDE THAT NO MAN COULD NUMBER is not to be distinguished from the 144,000. The apparent inconsistency is due to the fact that in verse 4 John was using a source, while this is his own free composition. Anyway, as we have seen, 144,000 is not meant to be taken literally, but indicates completeness. Here the size of the Church is emphasised rather than its completeness. We cannot tell whether the hymn which they sing is intended to have any poetic form (cf. 4. 11; 5. 12, 13). No care has been taken to distinguish from each other the various qualities ascribed to God and to the Lamb. They are just strung together indiscriminately, as it seems. Each of the qualities ascribed to God sums up some aspect of his being, something new about his relationship to men (see Introduction, p. 47, for a suggested analysis of one of these hymns). Each is, in a sense, an act of praise in itself. They are more like chapter headings to a hymn book. As such, they are deeply meaningful and will repay study.

The R.V. reading in verse 14 is to be preferred: THE GREAT TRIBULATION. John's readers would have no doubt at all about what he referred to. Some of them would be undergoing 'the great tribulation' as he wrote, the persecution of the Imperial authorities. 'The tribulation' was almost a technical term with the early Church: they had been warned to expect it as a sign of the end. See Mark 13. 19, where the word translated 'affliction' by the A.V. is the same as that which it translates 'tribulation'.

THEY HAVE WASHED THEIR ROBES AND MADE THEM WHITE
IN THE BLOOD OF THE LAMB. That is, they have undergone
that process of death and new life which Jesus by his coming
inaugurated for us and which enables us to have free communion with God. For John this process was exemplified
par excellence in martyrdom, and there is strong evidence
that he believed all Christians would eventually be martyred.
With verse 15 cf. 22. 3 and note p. 140. See also note on 21.
3, p. 139. For a discussion of John's picture of heaven
referred to in verses 16 ff., see notes on 22. 3, p. 140.

(b)

8 – 9; 11. 14-19; 13: The Seven Trumpets

The seven seals are now over, and, after the interlude of
ch. 7, the next set of judgments now begins—the seven
trumpets. They last till the end of ch. 13. This is section 4
(b) in the scheme on p. 22. We do not reach 4 *(c)*, the seven
vials (bowls) until p. 105.

The SILENCE IN HEAVEN ABOUT THE SPACE OF HALF AN
HOUR is one of those unexpected and effective details of
which John is such a master. It serves the double purpose of
heightening the awfulness of the seven trumpets when they
do sound, and of underlining the importance of the prayers
of the saints. Its immediate purpose in the narrative appears
to be to allow the prayers of the saints to be heard. It reminds
us that when all is said about God that can be said, nothing
has been said. In a sense God's infinite majesty and glory
is beyond all words, and sometimes the highest tribute we
can pay him is to remain in silent adoration before him.

We have seen in 6. 9, that the altar, which reappears in
verse 3 here, is the symbol of the connection between Christ's
sacrifice and the sacrificial lives and deaths of Christians.
The prayers of the saints are here offered on the altar,
because it is in prayer that the offering which the Christian's
day-to-day life should be, is focused and consciously offered
to God through Christ. The angel censing them as they are
offered signifies that he is making them acceptable to God.
The Jews of our Lord's day believed that it was the special

function of the Archangel Michael to offer Israel's prayers (see Dan. 12. 1),[1] and it is possible that John is Christianising this belief here. But we must not imagine that there is any suggestion of an angelic mediator, as if angels were semi-divine beings, intermediate in status between God and man. John always thinks of angels as 'fellow-servants' with Christians (Rev. 19. 10; 22. 8 f.). The object of the angelic intervention is to emphasise the absolute unity between the Church on earth and in heaven. Prayer is the common atmosphere which all Christians of all ages breathe. When the angel in verse 5 takes the censer and throws it on the earth it seems to mean that the prayers of the saints actually precipitate the judgments.

On the whole, the judgments which follow the seven trumpets seem to be more connected with what we would call 'natural causes'. As in ch. 16, they appear to be based on the plagues of Egypt in Exodus. Is John suggesting that 'natural' catastrophes can show up the good and bad qualities in man as surely as the humanly contrived disasters of the previous series? WORMWOOD is the proverbial symbol of bitterness. Hence it refers in verse 11 to the bitterness of spirit which the sin of man brings about. In verse 13 John inserts the first of three woes; the others are to be found in 9. 12 and 11. 14. They cannot be described as separate judgments, since all coincide with trumpet blasts. The object of the third woe (11. 14) seems to be postponed till ch. 13. Perhaps John found them in his materials and interwove them with the other judgments in order to heighten the horror of his narrative.

The exact significance of the locusts in ch. 9 is not clear. The locusts are not among God's creatures; they come from the abyss; so it may well be a picture of how God uses material evil, which he has not engineered, for his own purposes. A great plague would fit the picture well; if so, it reminds us that God is not the cause of illness and suffering.

In verse 1, I SAW A STAR FALL FROM HEAVEN simply means a great angel alighting on the earth. The abyss was tradition-

[1] Michael also prays for Israel in 1 Enoch.

ally the element hostile to God, which he had to overcome before creating the world (or, in an early version of the myth, setting in order a formless chaos; cf. Gen. 1. 2). Hence it came to be looked on as the abode of God's enemies, though only the temporary abode, as we see by the end of the book. It is the preliminary place of punishment of the fallen angels, demons, the Beast and false prophet, and the prison of Satan for a thousand years. ABADDON and APOLLYON in verse 11 mean 'Destroyer'. He must be one of the fallen angels whom we meet again in 12. 7. The four chained angels from the Euphrates go back to very ancient mythological sources, but here no doubt they refer to the expected Parthian invasion of the Roman Empire which was much in the air towards the end of Domitian's reign; the Euphrates was the boundary between the rival empires. The Emperor Trajan some ten years later conducted a series of very successful wars against Parthia. Verse 15 indicates that the time of this judgment is limited and controlled by God. On verse 20 it has been well said by one commentator that disasters seldom stir a man who disbelieves in a living and good God to confess him.

10 – 11. 13: *Second Parenthesis: the angel of the book; the Temple and the two Witnesses.*

The whole parenthesis seems to be intended to prepare us for the ultimate appearance of the Beast. (Whether we can say the Beast appears in 11. 7 is doubtful. It seems to be a prophecy, not a vision; but we are back again in the past tense in 11. 11 and the Beast makes a very definite appearance in 13. 1.) It is quite likely that John found the materials for this chapter in the sources he wished to use, and inserted it here as the most convenient place.

In verse 3 John apparently originally intended to give us yet another series of judgments called the 'seven thunders', but changed his mind.

In verse 6 THERE SHOULD BE TIME NO LONGER has no metaphysical significance. John is not trying to define eternity: he simply means 'there shall be no delay'. THE MYSTERY OF GOD in verse 7 means the working out of God's hidden purpose. 'Mystery' to us is usually something associated with the police court and the popular press, but in the New Testament it bears this nobler meaning; cf. Eph. 1. 9; Rom. 16. 25. The EATING OF THE BOOK in verses 9 ff. is taken from Ezek. 2. 8. 'Eating the book' means thoroughly understanding its contents. The events contained in this prophecy were apparently to be superficially favourable, but on deeper consideration would be seen to be unpleasant.

We have been prepared for the coming of some great event, the appearance of the Beast. His appearance in ch. 11 means that the final struggle and triumph of Christ is rapidly approaching. So there come on the scene two figures who are connected with what preceded the first coming of Christ. This is probably the sequence of thought which John's narrative follows. On analysis, however, ch. 11 is one of several places where John is using sources which he adapts and incorporates in his work. Verses 1-2 make up one fragment (see Introduction p. 37), and verses 3-13 the other. In its original form the source represented in verses 3-13 was probably purely a Jewish prophecy, uttered just before Jerusalem fell to the Romans in A.D. 70. It was meant to indicate that at the last minute the Jews would repent as a consequence of the preaching of two witnesses from heaven, and thus be supernaturally saved from their enemies.

John has, of course, adapted this prophecy for his own purpose. The two witnesses are, as in the original prophecy, Moses and Elijah (Elijah is identified by comparing verse 5 with 2 Kings 1. 10, and Moses by comparing verse 6 with Ex. 7. 19; cf. also Mark 9. 2-8). But in Revelation they are something more than that: they also stand for the Law and the Prophets, and they are represented as bearing witness to Christ. That the whole Old Testament pointed forward to Christ was one of the foundation stones of the early Christian message (cf. Luke 24. 27). Through the influence of the Devil (verse 7) the real meaning of the Law and the Prophets is rejected by God's own people, but with the triumph of Christ's resurrection the truth is vindicated (verse 11). Then a dreadful judgment falls upon the Jews as a result of this: the destruction of their city by the Romans.

A fuller explanation of verses 1-2 has been given in the Introduction, p. 37. Forty-two months in verse 2 means, of course, a period of $3\frac{1}{2}$ years. It had become in Jewish literature the traditional period for the triumph of evil. This was partly, no doubt, because $3\frac{1}{2}$ is half 7, and 7 is the perfect number; but it was also the period during which Antiochus Epiphanēs maintained an image of Olympian Zeus in the Temple at Jerusalem (see Introduction, p. 14). The Book of Daniel refers to this period, and the reference helped in the standardisation of $3\frac{1}{2}$ years as the duration of the evil power. (See Dan. 12. 7, where 'a time, and times, and half a time' means $3\frac{1}{2}$ years.) Verse 4 brings us back to the Book of Zechariah, one of the minor prophets, who lived about 520 B.C., just after the Jews had returned from exile in Babylon. Zechariah has a vision (Zech. 4) of two olive trees, one standing on each side of a golden candlestick. The candlestick represents God, who is supplying power and inspiration to Joshua, the High Priest at the time, and Zerubbabel, the native Jewish governor under the Persian King Darius. In Zechariah therefore the vision is intended to portray both Church and State working together for the reconstruction of Israel. That can hardly be John's purpose in view of the fact that, when he wrote, the State was actively persecuting the Church! He simply takes this vision as an example of how God does supply his divine power to chosen individuals, and uses it to show how especially marked out for divine favour these two witnesses were.

The Beast is very abruptly introduced in verse 7. This is one of the signs that John is using a source. The proper entry of the Beast occurs in ch. 13. The Beast was a stock figure in the Jewish literature concerning the Last Things which grew up in the century immediately before our Lord's time. (See Introduction, p. 16.) John wanted to use this particular source before he described the appearance of the Beast, hence the slight anomaly.

When one recalls the tremendous veneration the Jews had for Jerusalem 'the holy city', one realises the deep significance of verse 8. The phrase WHICH SPIRITUALLY IS CALLED SODOM OR EGYPT, WHERE ALSO OUR LORD WAS CRUCIFIED, is certainly an addition by our author to his source. It shows what a complete reversal of values Christianity brought about even in so Hebrew-minded a man as John. The city which in Ps. 48. 2 is called 'the joy of the whole earth' has become one with the traditionally wicked cities of the Old Testament, *because* it has crucified its Lord (cf. Wisdom 19. 14 ff.). Notice that in verse 13 THE REMNANT expresses remorse, not repentance (cf. 16. 15-17, and also Jas. 2. 19); they acknowledge God's power and realise that the working out of his judgments is in process.

11. 14-19: The Seventh Trumpet

These verses provide a brief recall of the main theme between the two parentheses 11. 1-13 and 12. The seventh trumpet really ushers in the events in ch. 13. These few verses give us a brief glimpse of the heavenly worship before we plunge again into the terrible struggle that is upon us. In verse 18 we get a hint as to how God's judgments work out: the destroyers are destroyed. It is the next thing to saying they destroy themselves (cf. Luke 6. 38). In verse 19 THE ARK OF HIS TESTAMENT refers no doubt to the New Testament, the new covenant or relationship established between God and man by the life and death of Christ. The old ark held the ten tables of stone, evidence of the old covenant made on Sinai (cf. Heb. 9. 1-2). So John permits us an anticipation of the triumph in heaven in verses 14-19. We today need not dismiss these verses as relating to a period far beyond our ken. With the death and resurrection of Jesus Christ the kingdoms of this world are in principle already become the kingdoms of God and of Jesus Christ. If it were not so we could not claim them as his by right as boldly as we do. Even today we can in some degree share in the rejoicing over the triumph of the power of God.

12: *Third Parenthesis: the Woman, the Child and the Dragon*

This parenthesis might almost be described as a 'flashback'. It takes us back to the events of the life and resurrection of Christ, and even farther back still to the Fall of the Angels. John put it in, no doubt, because the significance of ch. 13 could not be understood in all its depths unless one realised what had gone before. It is probably to modern eyes the most bizarre chapter in Revelation. We saw in the last chapter that John was making use of a special source; he does that here also, and an examination of his sources explains much that is difficult in this chapter. There are two sources here. The first is the story of the woman clothed with the sun. It begins at verse 1, is interrupted by verses 7-12, and is resumed in verses 13-16. This first source has its origin in pagan mythology. In the legends of Egypt, Babylon, and Greece we find the story of the goddess who was destined to bear a son who would rule the world, and was pursued by a dragon when she was about to bring forth. It was a well-known story in the ancient world; one might almost call it an international myth. It is, however, very probable that when John found it, it had already been given a Hebrew dress by some Jewish writer. It is most unlikely that John would have borrowed directly in this way from the paganism he abhorred. Some Jewish writer had conceived the notion of boldly claiming for the true God the well-known pagan story, and had made it apply to the birth of the expected Messiah. It was this Jewish version of the pagan myth that John used. The other source (verses 7-12), the story of war in heaven, is wholly Jewish. Strictly speaking, the source before John touched it consisted of verses 7-9; John added verses 10-12 when adapting it for his own purpose, as we shall see. Its beginnings can be traced in the Old Testament. It arose as an attempt to answer the most profound question which belief in a righteous God provokes: how did evil come into the world? Genesis gives at least a provisional answer: by the sin of Adam. Man, given free will by God, deliberately chose the bad rather than the good, hence his heritage of sin and suffering. But Jewish thinkers, concerned as ever with moral rather than metaphysical problems, came in time to see two flaws in this. It did not account for evil in nature, and it did not explain how man came to be tempted in the first place

(Genesis does not explain *why* 'the serpent was more subtil than any beast of the field', Gen. 3. 1). So gradually there grew up a belief in a pre-cosmic fall, the conception of a rebellion of angelic powers against God before the world was made, or at least before man was. (There is a hint of this in Ezek. 28. 11-17, where the king of Tyre is compared to the angelic cherub who dwelt in the paradise of God where the trees bore precious stones, but who fell through pride; cf. also Isa. 24. 21, where 'the host of the high ones' are rebellious angels.) Though this only puts the problem of the origin of evil a stage farther back, it does make it easier to understand how the *whole world*, nature as well as man, can have been affected (C. S. Lewis in his series of novels beginning with *Out of the Silent Planet* treats this theme very interestingly). It is important to realise that this theory of a pre-cosmic fall is not just the quaint conception of primitive minds, but a serious attempt to solve a great intellectual problem, one which still commends itself to some competent theologians today. It is this conception that John includes in his account of war in heaven.

We have yet to explain how John adapts and combines these materials. The first part of the pagan myth, verses 1-6, describes the birth and triumph of the Christ. The woman clothed with the sun is the Church; she is described as mother of the Christ because in the New Testament the Christian Church is always viewed as continuous with the Jewish 'church' before Christ, God's chosen community. This community therefore existed before Christ's birth and it was in the bosom of this community that he was born (cf. Isa. 54. 1-3; Acts 7. 38; Gal. 4. 26). The Dragon is the devil, who attempts to destroy the Christ by the hands of Pilate and the rulers of the Jews. But Christ is snatched up to heaven (the Resurrection and Ascension) and the Church escapes. Then comes the story of war in heaven (verses 7-12). John means to connect the triumph of Christ with the fall of the angels. By a bold sweep of the imagination he tells us, through the tremendous symbolism of the divine warfare, that the coming of God to earth in Christ and its consequences has confirmed and completed what happened when the angels became evil and were thrown down from the presence of God. As that Fall had a cosmic significance for evil, so this Incarnation has a cosmic significance for good. Through the symbol of Michael's warfare John sees Christ's victory on earth (cf. Luke 10. 18, and John 12. 31). As in verse 7 of the last chapter, so here, John's use of sources involves him in some anomalies. The myth of the woman clothed with the sun is not very well suited to John's purpose, as it leaves no room for Christ's life and death. And the fact that the triumph of Christ is connected with God's triumph over the evil angels is not clearly indicated by depicting the Archangel Michael as the leader of heaven's armies. John has tried to mitigate these anomalies by inserting verses 10-12.

We have had to say a good deal about John's use of sources in order to understand what he says to us, but we must not make the mistake (too common nowadays) of imagining that, when we have laid bare the sources a writer uses, we have in some way disposed of the truth or value of what he says. In fact, of course, every great writer has materials and sources which he uses (Aeschylus and Shakespeare are admirable examples). The important question is not What sources does he use? but What use does he make of them? Indeed, if we once get some idea of John's technique, the masterly way in which he adapts and combines his various sources will make us pay more, and not less, attention to what he is using those sources to express. We have already (Introduction, p. 34) seen something of his profound use of the Old Testament; now perhaps we are in a position to appreciate the way in which he uses Jewish speculations and even pagan traditions to place for us in their true cosmic perspective the central affirmations of Christianity.

The sun and the moon and the stars adorning the woman simply indicate the status of the Church. 'She was before all things, and for her sake all things were made' says *The Shepherd of Hermas*, an early Christian romance. Similarly the Dragon's casting the stars to earth in verse 4 indicates his power, as do his horns and crowns. The Dragon can boast a long lineage; he was originally identical with the abyss (see note on 11. 7). In Gen. 1. 2 the word for 'deep' is etymologically connected with Tiamat, the Chaos-dragon in Babylonian mythology, whom God had to destroy before creating the world. The next addition to his character comes when he was identified with the serpent in Gen. 3 (see verse 9: THAT OLD SERPENT). Finally he was also connected with the Satan of the O.T. In the O.T. itself Satan is hardly an evil character. He is simply the Recording Angel or Public Prosecutor in the Divine Court. His name means 'adversary' (see Job 1 and 2). But naturally his office soon brought him an evil reputation, and well before John's day he was thought of as himself an evil angel; not the necessary adjunct of divine justice, but THE ACCUSER OF OUR BRETHREN, one who tempted, and accused falsely.

In verse 7 a more accurate translation is: 'Michael and his angels had to fight against the dragon.' The SHORT TIME in verse 12 is in fact the whole course of human history, but 'a thousand years in thy sight are but as yesterday' (Ps. 90. 4). Eternity is on God's side, and he can afford to wait.

Commentators have perplexed themselves trying to guess what is meant by the wilderness in verse 14, as in verse 6; but this detail need not be pressed. It simply means that the Church survived the death of the Christ. The incident of the flood in verses 15 and 16 is no doubt there primarily because it was part of the original myth. If we follow out the meaning of the story as John uses it we may legitimately conclude that the flood incident refers to the attempts of the Jewish authorities in Jerusalem to stamp out Christianity when they had failed to dispose of Christ. Take the first sentence of ch. 13 with the end of verse 17 of ch. 12 and translate (following the R.V.) 'the dragon . . . went to make war with the remnant of her seed . . . and he stood upon the sand of the sea'. We must imagine that the Devil, having failed to stamp out the Church by local Jewish persecution, now summoned a much more dangerous ally, the Roman State. John's transition from his parenthesis (ch. 12) to his main theme in ch. 13 is skilfully done by this verse.

13: The Third Woe: The Satanic Trinity

We are still in Section 4 (*b*) in our scheme. We now return to our main theme. The symbolism of this chapter is taken mostly from Daniel (see pp. 35 and 39). John sees in his contemporary situation a parallel to that which faced the author of Daniel, and adopts the imagery of the older author accordingly. The Beast which John perceives rising from the sea we must take as representing first and foremost the Roman Empire. (Rome's communications with Asia Minor were, of course, by sea.) Its might and ruthlessness are symbolised in the bestial accoutrements of verse 2. But, as the Beast comes closer, John is able to give us a more exact description, and we realise that that Empire is summed up and completed in the figure of one of its worst rulers. In verse 3 we are told that one of the Beast's heads had a deadly wound that was healed. This refers to one of the Emperors, an Emperor who had been wounded to death, and whom John depicts here as coming to life again. In the year 68 B.C. the Emperor Nero, when he had been abandoned by the Imperial bodyguard, and while a rival at the head of a powerful army was rapidly approaching Rome, stabbed himself in the throat in one of his villas near the city. This had taken place nearly thirty years before Revelation was completed. But during those years the legend had grown up that Nero was not dead, but would return from the East with a vast army to overthrow the Roman Empire.[1] Moreover the reigning Emperor was then Domitian, who was a rival to Nero in savagery and licentiousness. He also resembled Nero in another significant respect: he persecuted the Church.[2] John therefore takes this current belief and

[1] This belief, against all the evidence, in the survival of famous or notorious figures in history is quite common. The medieval Emperor Barbarossa was believed to be still alive in a cave in Salamanca many centuries after his death. As recently as 1891 many Irishmen refused to believe that Charles Stuart Parnell was really dead. The legend ran that a coffin full of lead was carried at his funeral.

[2] The resemblance between Nero and Domitian was noticed by contemporary writers. Juvenal, Latin satirist of about A.D. 100, begins one of his poems 'While the last of the Flavii was still afflicting the tortured world, and Rome bowed her neck to a bald version of Nero . . .'; the reference is to Domitian.

uses it to symbolise the Roman Empire in its character as persecutor of the church. As we shall see later on, John sees Nero Redivivus as the overthrower of the Empire. But this is not till ch. 17.

The second Beast (verse 11) is the organised worship of the Emperor practised throughout the Empire, but especially in Asia Minor (see Introduction, p. 25). It was over this worship that conscientious Christians came into conflict with the Empire. The cult was a wealthy, popular, and powerful one, as is indicated in verses 12-15. John refers to this second Beast as *the false prophet* in 16. 13 and 19. 20 (cf. Deut. 13. 2). Both Emperor and Emperor-worship are represented as being directly instigated by the Devil in his war against the Lamb.

As we study the details of this chapter there is one astonishing feature which gradually becomes apparent: Satan has produced a parody of the divine dispensation. The Dragon, the First Beast, and the Second Beast (each of the last two proceeding from the one before it), correspond to the Trinity.[1] Nero Redivivus is Satan Incarnate.[2] There is even a death and resurrection in the death and return of Nero (cf. 'the Lamb that had been slain'). Even more, Satan produces a world church, with certain marks of its own to distinguish its members from the rest of the world (verse 16), cf. the sealing of the faithful in 7. 3. Finally, it is worth observing that just as the divine dispensation is called a 'mystery' in 10. 7, so there is the 'mystery of iniquity' which belongs to the Roman Empire (see 17. 5).

In all this John is not merely indulging in bizarre and fantastic speculations. He is concerned with matters of fundamental importance for the history of the world and the understanding of the way in which God deals with man.

---

[1] The doctrine of the Trinity as we know it today had not, of course, been explicitly formulated in John's time.

[2] John also no doubt saw in the Beast the figure of Antichrist, the great opponent of the Messiah who was traditionally expected to appear at the end of history. The early Christians shared this expectation, cf. 1 John 2. 18, 22; 2 John, verse 7; also Mark 13, 22. Our John never actually uses the name Antichrist, but the Beast has every mark of that figure.

With truly inspired insight he has laid bare for us principles of life which prove themselves true again and again in the course of world history. The profound thought which lies behind these tremendous pictures is that man is made to worship some absolute power, and that if he does not worship the true and real Power behind the universe, he will construct a god for himself and give absolute allegiance to that. It seems indeed that John goes farther than this, and asserts that man will always tend to worship some sort of Trinity and to adore some sort of Incarnation, even if he rejects the true Trinity and the true Incarnation. If so, we must confess that the events which culminated in World War 2 have provided an amazing confirmation of John's insight. In John's day men worshipped the god of power, incarnate in the Roman Emperor, propagated by the Imperial Cultus. In our day we have seen millions of civilised Europeans giving wholehearted allegiance to the god of the Germans, incarnate in Adolf Hitler, propagated by the Nazi Party; and millions of Japanese living and dying for the god of Japan's destiny, incarnate in the Mikado, and propagated by state Shinto-worship. Dozens of minor parallels could be culled from history, from the divine status of the Egyptian Pharaohs to the syncretistic Emperor-worship invented by Akbar, Mogul Emperor of India in the seventeenth century. All are summed up in this brilliant chapter of Revelation. It is as if Jesus' words 'Ye cannot serve God and Mammon' were being illustrated on the stage of world history. Revelation throughout is concerned with a problem which has become desperately acute in the atomic age, the problem of power. Men will always give their allegiance to some sort of power, so John tells us in this chapter, and in the last analysis it is always a choice between the power that operates through inflicting suffering, the power of the Beast, and the power that operates through accepting suffering, the power of the Lamb.

In verse 1 it is better to take the seven heads and the ten horns as a general indication of a complete series of powerful Emperors. On this problem see the note on 17.11, pp. 114-15. The better reading is 'names of blasphemy' (R.V.) as in verse 5; John means the titles whereby the Emperors claimed divine power and authority. Domitian liked to be called 'our God and Lord'. In verse 6, Charles has a probable suggestion. He says that the Greek word here translated 'tabernacle' is meant to render a Hebrew one which means 'God's glory.' Hence he would translate: 'to blaspheme his name and his glory'.

In verse 8 FROM THE FOUNDATION OF THE WORLD can be taken grammatically either with WRITTEN IN THE BOOK OF LIFE or with THE LAMB SLAIN, and either is perfectly possible theologically. In the first case John is asserting, in common with other New Testament writers, that those who have responded to God's calling and entered his service in the Church are taking their part in a divine plan which embraces the whole course, not only of human history, but also of the history of the universe. In the second case he is asserting that, God's character of self-giving love (now revealed in Christ) being what it is, and the consequences of man's endowment with free will being what they are, it was inevitable that the Son of God should take flesh and die. In neither case are we committed to a mechanical predestinarianism (cf. Rom. 16. 25-26; Eph. 1. 4).

In verses 9 and 10 John inserts a most appropriate warning. It affirms the principle upon which God's government of the world turns: sin must bring its reward of suffering and ultimate frustration. This is how God's wrath works out. Christian insight into history consists in holding on to this clue. It appears here no doubt to remind us that all power ultimately belongs to God and he is still in control even when evil seems omnipotent.

In verse 11 HE SPAKE AS A DRAGON probably means 'he spake as deceitfully as the Dragon speaks', who, as the Serpent, deceived Eve in Paradise. The image in verse 14 refers to the statues of the Emperor which all his subjects were obliged to worship. It seems likely that John means us to understand by verse 15 that all faithful Christians have been put to death. This is to some extent borne out by the subsequent course of his book. If so, it forms a strange contrast to the rosy picture of the Kingdom of God on earth which many modern Christians imagine that their faith justifies them in expecting. The mark on the hand and on the brow mentioned in verse 16 seems in fact to be borrowed from Judaism. The 'phylacteries' (small boxes containing texts from the Law) were bound on the brow and on the hand. But here and in 7. 3 there is a distinct reference to Ezek. 9. 4, where we have a grim picture of destroyers sent by God to slay all those who had not on their foreheads a mark. From the Hebrew of this passage it appears that the mark was the Hebrew Letter *tau*. In Ezekiel's time (and in John's) that letter would be written as a cross—X (Greek *chi*). Now there can be little doubt that John has this passage in mind here, and is thinking of the X of Christ's name. It is possible that he saw in this marking of the righteous in 7. 3 a correspondence with baptism or confirmation, in which a cross was made on the forehead of the new Christian. Here in the marking of the servants of the Beast John sees a parody of Christ's name and of baptism.[1]

The speculations as to the meaning of 666 in verse 18 throughout the history of the Church have been varied and innumerable, ranging from the Pope of Rome to Napoleon Bonaparte. Scholars are fairly well agreed by now that it can be legitimately interpreted by a traditional Hebrew cipher which would almost certainly be known to a man of John's background. When so decoded, it can without undue manipulation be made to render the words: *Neron Kesar*, Caesar Nero.

14: *Fourth Parenthesis: Vision of the Lamb on Mount-Sion and of the Son of Man in power*

Ch. 13 has described to us the course of the great war between the Beast and the Lamb. Now in ch. 14 we turn aside for the last time to consider in two visions the eternal background or meaning of the war. The first vision shows how those who are really faithful to God are vindicated by the conflict, and the second shows the working out of the

[1] We owe the reference to the Hebrew of Ezekiel to the Rev. R. P. C. Hanson.

consequences of the original rebellion against God which caused the war, and how they come back on the heads of those who are responsible for them. The division between the visions occurs at verse 6. Perhaps nowhere more clearly than in this chapter do we meet those conceptions and beliefs which the average Christian associates with Revelation and which he is inclined today to repudiate. So we must spend some time in an attempt to discover what those conceptions and beliefs really mean. But they are better dealt with under the verses where they occur.

As we saw in 7. 4, the 144,000 means the entire Christian Church. Since we are to understand that all faithful Christians have been martyred by this time, we must imagine that the whole terrestrial world is now pagan. It has been objected to this that in verse 4 these 144,000 are described as FIRST-FRUITS, indicating that there are many others yet to come. But Charles has shown good reason for the view that in the particular Hebraic Greek which John used 'first-fruits' had lost all sense of being a first or token offering, and simply meant an offering[1] (cf. the vulgar use of 'alibi' to mean any excuse, not necessarily an excuse that you weren't there). In the widest sense it is true that all Christians must die to this world; their calling is to be as self-sacrificial in their lives as any martyr.

The NEW SONG in verse 3 recalls 5. 9; several of the Psalms include the injunction to sing 'a new song' (Ps. 33. 3; 40. 3; 98. 1); it indicates a special act of praise for a special deliverance. The suggestion in verse 4 that only those who have never had intercourse with women can be saved is a truly astonishing one. If taken literally it means that only male celibates can be saved! It is, of course, a dangerous proceeding simply to excise whatever seems unpalatable, but it does seem to be justified here. We know that soon after the age of the Apostles the notion crept into the Church that there was something defiling about the physical side of marriage (an unsuccessful attempt was made at the Council of Nicaea in A.D. 325 to have celibacy as such recommended).

[1] Forty out of sixty-six times in the Greek O.T. it merely means offering.

It seems likely that some ascetically minded scribe took the opportunity of inserting his propaganda into Revelation before the text had become standardised. But there is no manuscript evidence for this. On verse 7 F. D. Maurice comments: 'Take away the fear of God and he whom you worship contracts to your own dimensions. Only if the love of God were contracted would the horror of separation from him be less.'

Before the explanation of the darker side of the war, which begins in verse 8, the world, now entirely heathen, is given a last chance to repent. This EVERLASTING GOSPEL is not, apparently, *the* gospel of the life, death and resurrection of Christ. The world has had an opportunity of hearing that in the Church, and has rejected it. It seems to be rather a last appeal to all men to recognise the true God, both from the effects of disobeying him which history shows us (THE HOUR OF HIS JUDGMENT, verse 7), and from his works which always witness to him (HIM THAT MADE HEAVEN AND EARTH, etc.). It is the negative side of 'Believe me for the very works sake' (John 14. 11).

For fuller light on verse 8 see the notes on ch. 17. This passage (verses 8-12) brings us face to face with one of the great stumbling-blocks in Revelation to the modern Christian—its doctrine of hell. It certainly *sounds* vindictive and unchristian to a degree; but it is only fair to examine it more closely before we let our immediate feelings determine our judgment. The first thing to do is to discover the meaning of the very symbolic language which John uses. There are three main figures which he uses in verses 8-20: THE CUP OF INDIGNATION (wrath) THE FIRE AND BRIMSTONE of hell, and the VINTAGE of God's judgment. The vintage we may leave to be dealt with under verses 14-20. The cup of wrath is a conception taken from the Old Testament; one could well paraphrase it 'destiny of suffering'. Thus the anonymous prophet of Israel's exile whose works are incorporated in Isa. 40 – 55 declares that God has taken 'the cup of fury' out of Israel's hand and put it into the hands of her enemies (Isa. 51. 17-23). By this he means that Israel's lot of (deserved) suffering and adversity is now to be reversed.

Jesus speaks of his destiny to die on the Cross as 'this cup' (Mark 14. 36). The contrast in this passage between THE WINE OF THE WRATH OF HER FORNICATION (Babylon, verse 8) and THE WINE OF THE WRATH OF GOD (verse 10) means that, whereas Rome has inflicted a destiny of suffering (wrath) and degradation (fornication) on the nations of the world, now she is herself to suffer such a destiny at God's hands. Next we must remember that John cannot possibly have meant literal fire and literal brimstone in verse 10. Most intelligent people will admit that his language throughout the rest of his work is symbolical (e.g. in his descriptions of heaven). It would be totally unfair to take him literally here, and here only. Fire and brimstone are the traditional symbols for the fate of those who persistently reject God. We must understand, then, by verses 10 and 11, that those who reject God undergo some form of deserved suffering. But we can say more about their suffering than that; this torment John describes as the wrath of God. Now throughout Revelation we have seen ample reason for regarding the wrath of God as the disastrous consequences of sin working themselves out on those who have deliberately incurred them. If men persist in living contrary to the structure of God's universe they must suffer. So we are perfectly justified here in saying that this picture of wrath and hell means nothing more nor less than the terrible truth that the sufferings (the exact nature of which we cannot expect to understand) of those who persist in rejecting God's love in Christ are *self-imposed, self-incurred, self-perpetuated.* It is not a picture of an angry tyrant arbitrarily punishing those who have offended him with physical torture. It is the assertion, by means of traditional symbolism, that the most terrible thing that can happen to any human being is deliberately to turn away from the highest Good. This conclusion is supported by two minor pieces of evidence: THEY HAVE NO REST DAY NOR NIGHT (verse 11) echoes 'they rest not day and night' of 4. 8 (the same words in Greek). In ch. 4 this describes the voluntary worship of the angelic hosts, obeying the true law of their nature. In this chapter the phrase describes the deliberately chosen destiny of those who have turned against their true nature, but are in their very rebellion manifesting God's laws. The other piece of evidence consists in the coincidence of 14. 12 with 13. 10. In 13. 10 we saw that 'the faith and patience of the saints' means their ability to understand this working out of God's rule among men, his wrath and his love. So here it is only the saints, who understand God's love as well as his wrath, who can understand the true significance of the fire and the brimstone and the smoke.

But what about IN THE PRESENCE OF THE HOLY ANGELS AND IN THE PRESENCE OF THE LAMB (verse 10)? Does this not seem to suggest the repulsive idea that the saved in heaven witness, and perhaps enjoy, the sufferings of the damned? Now it certainly was a traditional belief among the Jews of Jesus' time that the redeemed would witness the torment of the wicked. It arose apparently from a misreading of the Hebrew of Isa. 66. 24, where 'and they shall be an abhorring unto all flesh' was misread as 'and they shall be in full view of all flesh'. But we cannot take this literally in Revelation any more than we can take fire and brimstone literally. What the phrase in verse 10 does is to remind us that the terrible condition of the wicked is caused directly by their relation to God. They have rejected God, and this means that they have rejected God's love in Christ. It is because they are destined to be sons of God in Christ and have refused to be sons of God that they have torment, that they have chosen thus to torment themselves. Their torment consists precisely in refusing to be members of the Lamb, fellow members with the angels. That is what 'in the presence of the Lamb' means. Their torment, says John, is FOR EVER AND EVER; that is because God will never intervene to *force* those who reject him to turn back. God's respect for man's free will never breaks down. God will do everything to win man back to him voluntarily—he has shown us that in the Lamb. But the inevitable consequences of this eternal love of his is that he will eternally treat us as persons. And if a man eternally persists in refusing him, he will never violate his personality. This does not forbid us to believe that God's persistent love will outlast the persistent refusal of any soul he has created, however obdurate. With verse 13 cf. 20. 12 and 13, and see p. 129.

Next we must turn to the difficult verses 14-20. The first thing to observe is that probably verses 15-17 were not written by John. If they are left out the whole scene is much clearer. On any interpretation verse 17 seems meaningless; there is nothing for the angel mentioned here to do. There is some evidence that very shortly after John finished Revelation his work fell into the hands of an editor, probably because John was dead. The editor may have inserted verses 15–17 in order to make the passage correspond more closely with Joel 3. 13, which it certainly does recall.

We have, then, in verses 14 and 18-20 a picture of the judgment of Christ. It is closely connected with the picture of hell which it follows and may be looked on as a fuller explication of the part which the Lamb plays in that scene. The figure is that of the vintage, and the vintage, like the harvest, is a symbol throughout the Bible of one of the deepest truths that the Bible has to convey: 'by their fruits ye shall know them'. Good must go on producing good, and evil, evil, till both have become perfectly obvious—and that becoming obvious is called the judgment. Nowhere is this truth more emphasised than in our Lord's teaching recorded in the Gospels. We think of the parable of the tares; but an even more striking parallel to this passage is Mark 4. 29, where almost the same phrase is used, 'put in the sickle' as in verse 18 here. In the Gospels the figure is always of the wheat harvest; we may conjecture that John preferred the wine vintage here because of its association with blood, and he believed that this great harvest of blood was already beginning to be gathered in the world of his day. John is telling us here more clearly perhaps than anywhere else that the rule of God is not arbitrary, but works exactly according to cause and effect in the moral sphere as much as in the material. We may be horrified at the picture of blood up to the horses' bridles, but, after the experience of two world wars in one generation, many thinking people are much more ready to admit that the root cause behind this terrible effusion of blood is not ignorance, or social conditions, but sin, the breaking of God's fundamental laws. They have seen in the history of the last twenty-five years the winepress of the wrath of God.

But John does not leave it at that. The being who holds the sickle is ONE LIKE UNTO THE SON OF MAN; it is the judgment of Christ. And in verse 20 we are given a hint which is more fully developed in 19. 11-16; the winepress is trodden WITHOUT THE CITY. The city is Jerusalem, and John is surely reminding us that Jesus was crucified outside Jerusalem. Compare Heb. 13. 10-15, where Christians are bidden to go forth to Jesus 'without the camp, bearing his reproach'. John is giving us just a glimpse of the amazing claim of Christianity that the way God judges his enemies is not by killing them but by suffering at their hands. The judgment which each great crisis in history brings, whereby the good and the evil in each situation is shewn up, is to be understood in the light of that one great judgment-act of God when the Son of God died on a cross 'without the city'. (See also Introduction, pp. 37 and 38.)

The space of 1,600 furlongs in verse 20 is probably chosen to indicate completeness of extent. Four is the complete number of extent, covering the four points of the compass (as seven is the complete number of quality); the square of four indicates entire completeness. It is multiplied by 100 as a sign of greatness, but note that this is not so great as the numbers in, or the size of the heavenly city, where the multiplier is 1,000 (ch. 7 and 21). The entire population of the world is involved in this divine judgment. We may well quote at the end of this chapter F. D. Maurice's remark that in Revelation God's highest blessings are revealed in punishments which look like curses.

(c)

15 - 16: The Seven Vials (Bowls)

Now that the great war in heaven has been described and explained, John here inserts his last series of judgments upon the world. They form the link between the account of the war and the judgment of the Beast (represented by the harlot). The reader will realise that we have reached 4 (c) in our scheme on page 22 of the Introduction. We may indeed wonder why John should want to insert this passage at all. Surely we have had enough of these judgments? The reason is probably simply that John had these two chapters (not in chapter form of course; our Biblical chapter divisions were invented at the time of the Renaissance) among the materials before him, and he decided that this was the most convenient place to fit them in. One must take what John offers as one finds it; there is always something of value hidden in it. These plagues differ from the other two series (the seven seals, 6. 1 – 8. 2; and the seven trumpets, 8. 6 – 11. 15) in that John probably means us to understand that they are inflicted upon an entirely heathen world. All the Church has been martyred, and it is this martyr host that we meet in verse 2.

15: The Preparation for the Last Judgments

In verse 1 John gives us himself at least a hint as to why these seven last plagues should occur. They fill up the wrath of God. That is to say, the consequences on the stage of history of man's breaking of God's laws have not yet been fully worked out. The SEA OF GLASS in verse 2 refers to 'the sea of glass' in 4. 6. There it represented the element of distance of God from man, the fact that the Creator must always be different from the creature, the unapproachability of God even in the midst of the eternal worship of heaven. Now the significant detail is added that fire is mingled with the glass. In that fire the whole difference which the Incarnation made to the God-man relationship is implied. It recalls God's inflexible opposition to sin, the consequences of man's rebellion against God, and the Cross on which Jesus as Man endured the consequences of sin. Between 4. 6 and this verse lies the whole drama of redemption and damnation.

The Song of Moses in verse 3 is to be found in Ex. 15. It is the song he is traditionally supposed to have sung after Israel had crossed the Red Sea in safety from Egyptian pursuers. John does here what one often finds in the N.T.—he refers back to the great divine deliverance at the beginning of Israel's history in order to enhance the far greater victory which Christ won for all mankind. When Jesus spoke of the New Covenant in the Upper Room he was pursuing the same line of thought. That is why THE TEMPLE OF THE TABERNACLE OF THE TESTIMONY appears in verse 5. 'The tabernacle of the testimony' (Num. 1. 50) was the place where access could be had to God when Israel was journeying in the wilderness. It contained the tablets of the Old Covenant. John means to say that, by reason of this new and greater deliverance, God's presence is now accessible to all in the new covenant relationship which is through Jesus Christ.

ALL NATIONS SHALL COME (verse 4). Though the Church has been slain, there is still a chance for the nations—a chance which some of them apparently take, to judge by 21. 24. But we must not press the chronology too closely, and there is surely here an echo of the world-wide mission of the Church.

16: The Last Judgments

We can only guess at the meaning of most of these judgments. Taken literally, they are not very impressive: boils, heat, darkness—painful enough, but scarcely what we should expect as the preparation for the great judgment of Rome which follows. We are probably safe in concluding that they are meant to be taken symbolically, though the symbolism itself is often a matter of conjecture. The first, third, and fifth plagues are taken from the plagues of Egypt. Most of the others consist of the signs which were traditionally expected before the Last Days.

It is possible that the first three plagues represent man's misuse of the earth's natural resources. The sore (caused by dust in the case of the Egyptians, Ex. 9. 9) may represent a plague caused by unhealthy living conditions. The second plague perhaps gives us a picture of the sea after a great sea-battle, the waters, as the Greek poet Aeschylus says, 'blossoming with corpses'. The third plague would then represent generally the misuse of the great element of water for man's destruction. It is even possible that we can add the fourth plague to this in verse 8, and say that this represents the misuse of fire. This scheme would come in very appropriately here: the Church, witness to God's law, having been removed from the world, men forget even the natural use and purpose of God's gifts (quite apart from ignoring his supernatural gift, Jesus Christ) and turn his works to their own destruction (cf. Rom. 1. 18-25 of the world *before* Jesus Christ). Verse 7 gives us the comment of the martyred church in heaven (as always the altar represents the martyrs). The comment is not unlike that which many people are making today about the atom bomb: THOU HAST GIVEN THEM BLOOD TO DRINK. God has allowed us to discover one of nature's greatest secrets, and we look like celebrating the event in blood.

The fifth plague in verse 10 represents the spiritual darkness of the Roman Empire: cf. Wisd. 17. 21, where the darkness of the Egyptians is spoken of as foreshadowing their spiritual darkness. It is not clear why darkness should cause pain. Perhaps there is the suggestion of yet another Egyptian plague, that of the boils; see Ex. 9. 8 f.

The sixth plague (verses 12-16) describes the preparations for the last great conflict between good and evil. It actually takes place in 19. 11 ff., and in 20. 7 ff. we have the still greater conflict at the end of the millennial reign. As we have seen (9. 14) the overthrow of the Roman Empire was expected to come about through an invasion from the east. The frogs represent generally the ability to deceive by means of superstitions and lies. Modern propaganda, as unscrupulously used by the totalitarian states, would certainly figure in this picture. Verse 15 seems out of place here: it is one of his seven beatitudes and may possibly belong to 3. 3. The conception of the last great battle between good and evil was part of the traditional Jewish belief about the Last Things. It is a profound myth, witnessing to the reality of good and the seriousness of evil. Hebrew belief in God's nature was such that it was not content to look on life as an unending conflict between good and bad as in

Persian religion. Because God was both righteous and almighty he must eventually overcome evil. We may be grateful to John for incorporating this particular myth into Christianity. Curiously enough, no one knows for certain what the name ARMAGEDDON means. It might mean 'mountain of plagues' or 'mountain of Megiddo'; but as Megiddo was a plain, this does not prove very illuminating. In Judg. 5. 19 (a very old song dealing with the triumph of Barak and Deborah) Megiddo is spoken of as a place where kings fought; here, for example, Saul was overthrown and here Josiah fell at the hands of Pharaoh Necho (2 Kings 23. 29); and in Zech. 12. 11 it is a place where the ritual mourning connected with the worship of Rimmon was carried on. In the latter case it would easily be associated with devils in John's mind.

The events following the opening of the seventh vial are immediately preparatory to the judgment of Rome which follows in ch. 17. Babylon's being divided into three parts probably signifies the crumbling of the Roman Empire.

V

THE FALL OF ROME, THE FINAL BATTLE, AND THE CAPTURING OF SATAN

(Ch. 17 – 20. 3)

JOHN is now approaching the climax of his narrative. He has completed his three series of judgments: the seals, the trumpets and the vials (bowls). The suspense has been built up until finally in 16. 19 he reaches the overthrow of Babylon (Rome), which has been hailed in advance in 14. 8. This was the supreme interest of his readers. Rome was the awe-inspiring Empire which was persecuting Christians. In what way could this monstrous evil be overthrown and God's righteous power and purpose be vindicated? John has so far shown that there will be no escape from personal danger for the Christian. The price of loyalty will be martyrdom. But he has also shown that this colossus has feet of clay and its overthrow will be swift and sure. Its wickedness will over-reach itself. Moreover, its overthrow will be the signal for God's final judgment on evil. John is now going to deal more fully with these events, to expand the latter part of ch. 16 and describe how Rome and its Empire is to be destroyed by an invasion from the east, and how the invaders are in turn destroyed by the Messiah in a final battle. Ch. 17 is an explanation of the destruction of Rome; ch. 18 a paean of triumph over its destruction; and ch. 19 begins by detailing the rejoicing in heaven over the defeat of Rome, and ends with a brief description of the final battle on earth, at the end of which in ch. 20. 1-3 Satan is bound for a thousand years during the millennium. During this time, the faithful Christians who have been martyred will reign with Christ. Then comes the Last Judgment and the new heaven and the new earth which John describes in ch. 21 and 22.

17: Further Account of the Fall of Rome

John's traditional apocalyptic images can hardly signify all he wishes to say in this chapter and, while his main meaning is clear, there is confusion about the details. We can agree with Kiddle that 'with the exception of the first five verses, ch. 17 is one of the least effective passages in Revelation. It displays most of the disadvantages of apocalyptic style and few of its advantages. The reason is that its purpose is to explain and not to inspire; the language of apocalyptic is as ill-suited to a pedestrian venture of this sort as, let us say, Shakespearian blank verse would be to the fashioning of a Shakespearian commentary'.

17. 1-6: The Vision of the Woman upon the Beast

ONE OF THE ANGELS WHICH HAD THE SEVEN VIALS (bowls) links this scene with the preceding chapter. THE GREAT WHORE (R.V. harlot) has not appeared before and so she is described. The subject of the chapter is the judgment of the whore, but most of it is taken up with describing the Beast who is both associated with her and yet is to be the means of her overthrow; this is the cause of the complications in the chapter. The title 'whore' is taken from Nahum 3. 4, where it is applied to Nineveh, the capital of the Assyrian Empire, and from Isa. 23. 16, where it is used of the commercial seaport of Tyre. Now John uses it of Rome, as he explains in verse 18. The MANY WATERS on which she sits aptly hit off Babylon in Jer. 51. 13, but are literally not appropriate to Rome; so in verse 15 John says they stand for PEOPLES AND MULTITUDES, AND NATIONS, AND TONGUES over whom Rome reigns and with whom THE KINGS OF THE EARTH HAVE

COMMITTED FORNICATION (verse 2). All this language of profligacy is familiar in the O.T. prophets in describing sin, especially the sin of the Israelites and of their holy city Jerusalem in forsaking their God and 'playing the harlot' by their disobedience to his will. This disobedience shewed itself in public and private unrighteousness, and in following the corrupt practices of the gods and goddesses of neighbouring peoples (see particularly Ezek. 16 and 23). Rome is the apotheosis of it.

John is carried away in an ecstatic vision IN THE SPIRIT (cf. 1. 10 and 4. 2) INTO THE WILDERNESS, a curious echo of another vision in the book of Isaiah, the doom of Babylon in Isa. 21. There he sees a woman sitting upon A SCARLET COLOURED BEAST, FULL OF NAMES OF BLASPHEMY, the political power of Rome. The woman is dressed in PURPLE AND SCARLET, purple being the royal colour and signifying the Imperial claims, whilst scarlet is the colour of sin (Isa. 1. 18); the names of blasphemy are the claims to divinity made by the Emperors and inscribed all over the empire in public places, on statues, temples, and public buildings. A further interpretation of the Beast is given in verses 8 and 11, where he becomes the resurrected Nero, who is to gather the Kings of the East and destroy Rome (see below). This is the complicated part of the chapter. John's point is that, as in Ezekiel's prophecy over Jerusalem, Rome's lovers will turn against her. Her lovers are the Beast and the kings of the earth (verse 2) and they will turn and rend her (verse 16 f.). So John makes the Beast stand at one and the same time for the Empire and the power that will overthrow it. The SEVEN HEADS are explained in verse 9 ff. and the TEN HORNS in verse 12 ff. Here again John introduces a confusion by making the heads stand both for the seven mountains on which Rome is built and also for seven kings with whom the Beast is associated (see below on verse 10 ff.). The horns are the ten kings; as we shall see, they are Parthian satraps who are to be associated with Nero.

In verses 4 and 5 we are given a further account of the pomp and luxury of Rome (a reference to Jer. 51. 7), and of her name which was on her forehead (cf. the mark of the

Beast in 13. 16) 'by way of a symbol', as Moffatt translates
MYSTERY. Rome had already been called Babylon in the N.T.
in 1 Pet. 5. 13, an interesting change of view from that of
Paul in Rom. 13. Up to the time Paul wrote, the Roman
authorities had on the whole given the early Church protection from the hostility of the Jews, as we can see from Acts;
but now with the growth of Emperor-worship the situation
had changed radically, as verse 6 reminds us. The saints are
the martyrs; both words refer to a single class (cf. 7. 13 f.).
John WONDERED at the enormity of the evil summed up in
his vision WITH A GREAT WONDER (R.V.; ADMIRATION in A.V.
is misleading to us today). How long could God possibly
allow it to exist? The angel proceeds to show John its doom.

17. 7-18: Explanation of the Vision, and the overthrow of the Woman

The Beast now becomes the risen Nero; he WAS, AND IS
NOT, AND SHALL ASCEND OUT OF THE BOTTOMLESS PIT (the
abyss, R.V.) The Beast recalls 13. 3 ff., and the bottomless
pit 9. 1 and 11. 7. The wounded head of 13. 3 has now come
to stand for the Beast as such. He will GO INTO PERDITION, a
prophecy which is fulfilled in 19. 20, but meanwhile THEY
THAT DWELL ON THE EARTH will WONDER, in the sense of
applauding and approving this ghastly travesty of God
(1. 8) and of Christ (1. 18) WHO WAS, AND IS NOT, AND YET
IS (better 'shall be' R.V. Margin). For the BOOK OF LIFE,
see 3. 5 and 13. 8.

John calls for the mind with WISDOM to interpret these
signs, and it is certainly needed, for the BEAST is now standing
for too many things for clarity. We have dealt with verse 9
above. In verse 10 the heads of the Beast are SEVEN KINGS
of whom FIVE ARE FALLEN, AND ONE IS, AND THE OTHER IS
NOT YET COME: AND WHEN HE COMETH, HE MUST CONTINUE
A SHORT SPACE; the beast is THE EIGHTH AND IS OF THE SEVEN.
These are the Roman Emperors, seven standing for the
complete series, the eighth being the risen Nero. He is thus
described as the head which was wounded to death and
healed (13. 3), as the Beast himself which had a wound by
the sword, and did live (13. 14), and now as the eighth head

who is of the seven. They are all quite appropriate descriptions. In reckoning the Emperors there is some difficulty in knowing where to start, but the most plausible method seems to be to count Augustus, Tiberius, Caligula, Claudius, and Nero as the five who are fallen, Vespasian as the one who is, and Titus as the one who is not yet come and is to continue only a short space. He was in fact an ailing man and reigned only from 79 to 81. This reckoning neglects the short and dubious reigns of Galba, Otho, and Vitellius. There are then three possibilities: (i) Domitian, in the last years of whose reign John wrote, is the eighth and is the equivalent of the monstrous Nero, which is unlikely in this context (contrast ch. 13), for it could hardly be said that 'he was and is not'; (ii) that John is using (imperfectly adapted) an earlier prophecy of the reigns of Vespasian or Titus, aided by the fact that pagan writers recognised a resemblance between Domitian and Nero; (iii) the number seven is symbolic of the sum total of Roman Emperors without specific references. In any event this verse remains a puzzle.

The ten kings of verse 12 go back to 16. 12, the kings of the East, Parthian leaders WHO HAVE RECEIVED NO KINGDOM AS YET, but obtain power for a brief period, ONE HOUR (cf. 18. 10, 17, 19), with the Beast. Nero gathers them to him to destroy Rome when he comes out of the pit (abyss). The number 10 comes from Dan. 7. 7. Having destroyed Rome, however, they are intending to MAKE WAR WITH THE LAMB and so verse 14 is really a parenthesis which looks to the final conflict before the millennium, described in 19. 19 ff. For the Lamb's title see 19. 16. Rome is to be overthrown by the product of the excesses of her own wickedness, and then those who overthrow her are in turn to be destroyed when they in blind folly make war on the Lamb, forgetting he is LORD OF LORDS AND KING OF KINGS. Meanwhile John is occupied with the fate of Rome. Nero and the Parthian satraps will strip her of her pomp, and destroy her, and in doing so they will think they are accomplishing their own purposes, as did the Assyrians of old (Isa. 10. 5 ff.), but in fact they are carrying out God's purposes (verse 17), and, like Assyria, they are going at the same time to their own destruction. Then the WORDS OF GOD will be accomplished (R.V.; fulfilled, A.V.).

18: The Doom-Song on Babylon (Rome)

For a discussion of the use of the O.T. in this chapter see section 9 of the Introduction. Here John's method of allusion without quotation of more than a few consecutive words together is seen at its height. It is a magnificent chapter which rolls off the tongue in sonorous, exultant phrases when read aloud, with the refrain IN ONE HOUR sounding like the solemn and regular tolling of a bell. So many echoes of doom-songs to be found in Isaiah, Jeremiah, and Ezekiel haunt the chapter that it is hard to get the full force of John without reading the key passages which he has at the back of his mind. Babylon, Tyre, Nineveh, the proud cities of the past, had come to an end, and now there was Rome, the quintessence of them all. She combined the political power of Babylon, against which the O.T. prophets of the exile period primarily directed their polemic, with the position of a commercial centre like Tyre whose iniquities particularly roused Ezekiel. Her destruction meant the divine judgment on civilisation as a whole organised apart from God, what the Fourth Gospel calls 'the world'. The very thought of the magnitude of it gives rise to a certain respect for Rome in John's mind. We find here something that does not occur elsewhere in Revelation: a certain sense of Rome's greatness, of its splendid vices even in the doom which its own folly has brought upon it. John gives us a series of pictures, drawn primarily from these O.T. sources, and the tenses switch bewilderingly from past and present to future as he contemplates what has already happened in the progress of his own narrative, but which, in the counsels of God, will shortly come to pass. Its doom is so certain that John can describe it happening in various pictures for which the tense sequence is irrelevant. Similarly, he can call God's people to come out of her (verse 4) although in the progress of his narrative all Christians have been slain; once more he is extolling that spirit in the churches which he has shown in ch. 2 and 3 to be necessary if they are to witness faithfully to their Gospel. It is a repetition of the message he has already delivered in those chapters. The civilisation which John dared to write about seemed to the outward observer secure enough and the benefits it provided for humanity solid. Where most would have been dismayed at the thought of its fall, John is serenely confident and regards that fall as due to its own wickedness. In the age of atomic power it is obvious to all that our civilisation is in danger. Yet it is not possible for Christians to regard its possible overthrow with the same detached exultation as John. Unlike his day, when the Church had little or no responsibility for public affairs, in ours the Church has been deeply involved in large parts of that civilisation. Judgment on it is to a large extent judgment on the house of God (1 Pet. 4. 17). While grasping the permanent truths of John's insight into the divine working in history and overcoming of evil, each generation has to work out for itself the bearing of John's message on its own particular time.

18. 1-3: Announcement of Rome's fall

That which was described at the end of the previous chapter is now said to be accomplished. The angel, like that of 14. 6, is undefined; the EARTH IS LIGHTENED WITH HIS GLORY as God lightens the earth in Ezek. 43. 2, and he echoes the cry over Babylon in Isa. 21. 9 as ch. 14. 8 has already done. John always adds THE GREAT to the O.T. description of Babylon to indicate the overwhelming importance of Rome. She is to be the haunt of foul spirits and birds (cf. Isa. 13. 21 and 34. 13-15, the latter referring to Edom) because the whole earth—kings and merchants—has been seduced and made drunk by her vicious ways (delicacies A.V., wantonness R.V., luxury R.V. Margin), as Tyre had misled them of old (Ezek. 27. 33).

18. 4-8: Christians to come out of the doomed city

This was the cry of prophecy against Babylon in Jer. 50. 8 and 51. 6, 45, and in Isa. 48. 20 and 52. 11 (which Paul quotes in 2 Cor. 6. 17). Her heaped-up sins have reached to heaven, and the prophet's voice asks heaven to reward her as she rewarded (R.V. rendered, and 'you' omitted, a reference to Jer. 50. 29), and then to double it (cf. Jer. 16. 18 against Jerusalem, and Isa. 40. 2). The iniquities with which she filled her cup (17. 4) have now turned into THE WINE OF THE WRATH OF GOD. Zeal for the vindication of God's righteousness and O.T. prophecy have run away with John here, for the N.T. revelation as a whole does not allow us to think of God as exacting double punishment for sin, or even the precisely equal retribution of verse 7. Rome's supreme sin was to imagine that she was her own mistress with no higher law than her own to obey, an attitude taken by empires before and since. With verse 7 compare especially Isa. 47. 7 ff., and Ezek. 27. 3. Her false security is rudely shattered IN ONE DAY.

18. 9-20: Lament of the Kings, Merchants, and Seafarers

This whole section is based on Ezekiel's vision of the judgment of Tyre (Ezek. 26 and 27) and needs little comment. The kings who had been associated with Rome (17. 2; 18. 3) BEWAIL and LAMENT not through sympathy for her fate but because of the overthrow of the stable world on which they had depended. THYINE WOOD in verse 12 is scented wood, like cedar. SOULS OF MEN in verse 13 is better 'lives of men' as R.V. Margin. In verse 14 John breaks in as he probably did in verse 6. The lament of the seafarers follows closely that of Ezek. 27. 27-32. With verse 18 cf. 13. 4, where men make the same half-admiring exclamation at the presence of evil in great power and splendour. After the threefold lament John calls on HEAVEN AND YE HOLY APOSTLES AND PROPHETS to rejoice (Jer. 51. 48), a summons which is answered in ch. 19 because GOD HATH AVENGED YOU ON HER (R.V. 'judged your judgment on her'). The prayer of the martyrs under the altar in 6. 9 has been answered, as has the continual prayer of the faithful against the wickedness of the oppressed such as we get in Ps. 43. 1.

18. 21-24: Babylon cast down

Once more we go back to one of the great sources of this chapter, Jer. 51. 63 ff., where the prophet performs a similar symbolical action to the strong angel. The picture of desolation which follows comes again from Ezek. 26. 13 and from Jer. 25. 10, and a frequent prophecy of Jeremiah about the evils that would fall on his own country (Jer. 7. 34; 16. 9; 25. 10). John lingers over the immensity of Rome's fall in one hour from overwhelming pride and power. The last verse of the chapter goes back to Jer. 51. 49 and, an alteration from the O.T., makes Rome symbolic of all the innocent blood shed on the earth. With this compare Jesus's judgment on Jerusalem in Matt. 23. 35.

19: The rejoicings of heaven at the marriage of the Lamb and the final battle between him and his adversaries

19. 1-10: Heaven rejoices at the marriage of the Lamb

In the two previous sombre and exultant chapters on the fall of Rome we have, with the exception of 17. 14, had no reference to the Lamb. Now with the overthrow of the harlot (WHORE, A.V.) John brings us sharply, as is his custom, from earth and its darkness to heaven and its glory. The heavenly choir, which has punctuated the series of judgments with its anticipatory praises of the eventual outcome, can now herald the accomplishment of the process. In ch. 4 and 5 they sing of the majesty of God and of the Lamb who is worthy to open the book; in 7. 9 ff. they hail the triumph, as yet unrealised, of the great multitude who will wash their robes and make them white in the blood of the Lamb; in 15. 2 ff. they are joined by these martyrs, now in heaven, and sing the song of Moses and of the Lamb, and in 16. 5 ff. they acknowledge the justice of the judgments of the vials (bowls) on the ungodly that remain. Now they can rejoice in response to the invitation of 18. 20 in the completion of a major stage in God's plan, the fall of Babylon (Rome).

ALLELUIA repeated four times in this passage is not found elsewhere in the N.T., though it occurs frequently in the Psalms as 'Praise ye the Lord', e.g. Ps. 146 – 150.

TRUE AND RIGHTEOUS are God's judgments (15. 3; 16. 7) because a corrupt civilisation, in John's view, had so sold itself to iniquity that it had become incapable of acknowledging the truth. Here as elsewhere in Revelation John regards the persecution of the Christians as the final sign of its iniquity. It could only be condemned and destroyed. Its punishment, therefore, fitted its crime (see 16. 7). HER SMOKE will rise up for ever, a sentence taken from Isa. 34. 10, and presumably to be interpreted as until the end of the millennial kingdom which John is to describe in the next chapter. In the new heaven and the new earth of ch. 21. f. there will be no room for Babylon's smoke. With verse 4. compare ch. 4. The voice of the next verse is presumably that of one of the living creatures; it echoes, as indeed the whole scene does, familiar Psalms like 113, 115. 13, and 135: a praise called for because THE LORD GOD OMNIPOTENT REIGNETH (1. 8; 11. 17). The first great stage in the destruction of evil had been when Satan was cast out of heaven; now his short time on earth (12. 12) had come to an end and he would scarcely survive the fall of Babylon. THE MARRIAGE OF THE LAMB IS COME. Again John gives us a forward glimpse, for the bride (the new Jerusalem, 21. 2) is not quite ready until Satan is finally overthrown and the last judgment is passed. Then 'the Spirit and the bride' can say 'come' (22. 17), and with that invitation the book ends. The thought goes back to O.T. times, where the people of Israel—the chosen people—are the bride of God (Hos. 2. 19 f.; Isa. 54. 5). In the N.T. Jesus uses the symbol of marriage in his parables of the kingdom of God, e.g. Matt. 22. 1-4; and Paul in Eph. 5. 22-33 works out his view of marriage on the basis of the revelation of Christ to his people. In the first instance this indissoluble union of Christ and the community which he has purchased (1. 5. f.) is enjoyed by the martyrs in the millennial kingdom; after the last judgment by all faithful Christians. One of the many angels tells John in verse 9 to write down the fourth beatitude of the seven (see 1. 3). Again there is a slight confusion in John's imagery, for the Christian is both the bride of Christ with the totality of the Church, and also the guest at his marriage (Matt. 22). Both are ways of expressing the close relationship of our Lord and his followers (see 21. 9). The next verse and a half form an aside which foreshadows 22. 8. John had rightly worshipped the Son of Man in 1. 17; in the light of this, notice the significance of WORSHIP GOD in this verse. Angel-worship, however, was quite another thing. There is little doubt that this is directed against angel-worship, which was found quite early in the church in Asia and is rebuked by Paul in Col. 2. 18 (see 22. 8). For John's brethren, the prophets, see 22. 9. Jesus and his revelation of God, which Paul calls 'the mind of Christ', is the content of the prophet's message as it is of what John has been told to write in his book: THE TESTIMONY OF JESUS IS THE SPIRIT OF PROPHECY.

19. 11-16: The Fifth Horseman of the Apocalypse, the Word of God

The moment of the final battle has arrived and the Messiah is to destroy the destroyers of Babylon, an event which was anticipated at the end of ch. 14. Heaven is wide open, and a horseman appears (cf. ch. 6). It is the Messiah, no longer a Lamb but a warrior, come to judge in righteousness (Isa. 11. 4). Nearly all the details are repetitions of earlier features, e.g. in the vision of ch. 1 and the details repeated in the letters to the seven churches. His VESTURE DIPPED IN BLOOD recalls Isa. 63. 1 ff. (The R.V. follows better MSS. evidence in reading 'sprinkled with blood'.) The difference between the figure in Isaiah and that of our Lord, however, is fundamental. In it lies the whole Christian gospel. Isaiah's warrior was red with the blood of his enemies. The Messiah was red with his own blood shed *for his enemies*. Behind all John's lurid pictures, we must not lose sight of that fact at the heart of the Messiah's judgments (cf. John 3. 16-19).

His NAME takes up 2. 17 and 3. 12. The martyrs who now join the angels in the heavenly army presumably know it. Others do not, for to know a name is to possess something of its power. The Messiah's name has power over heaven and earth, and whether John has let out the secret in verses 13 and 16 is not quite clear, but at any rate he is giving us a good idea of its significance. The WORD OF GOD takes us to the prologue of the Fourth Gospel (John 1. 1-14), which is fully discussed in all commentaries on that book. It signifies the Messiah's closeness to God. His was the creative power through whom God's Word found expression (see 3. 14). He it was who was 'made flesh and dwelt among us'. He is the KING OF KINGS, AND LORD OF LORDS (cf. 17. 14), titles which in the O.T. are given to God (e.g. Deut. 10. 17). He it is who can answer the blasphemous claims of the Beast. Verse 15 combines allusions to Isa. 11. 4 and Ps. 2. 9 with repetitions of 1. 16 and 14. 19 f.

19. 17-21: The Final Battle

The Messiah comes from heaven to battle like the word in Wisd. 18. 15 f. An angel STANDING IN THE SUN, i.e. mid-heaven, where the FOWLS are also later in the verse (birds, R.V.), calls the birds of prey to a grisly feast, a grim contrast to the marriage supper of the Lamb. The whole scene is based on the visions of Ezek. 38 and 39, especially 39. 17-20, where Gog from Magog assembles a barbarous multitude against the Jewish people and Jerusalem, but is completely defeated, and an era of peace opens. They are apocalyptic chapters, one of the earliest examples of what was to be a large literature (see Introduction, p. 13). John freely adapts it to his own use both here and in 20. 7 f.

The account of the final battle is extremely brief. It recalls the Armageddon scene of 16. 16. The Beast whom we first met in 13. 1 and the false prophet (who is the second Beast of 13. 11 ff., see introduction to ch. 13) are both seized and CAST ALIVE INTO THE LAKE OF FIRE (see 20. 14, an echo of Dan. 7. 11), and the rest are killed and presumably go to Hades to await the final judgment, which is described in the next chapter.

20. 1-3: Satan bound for 1,000 Years

Satan remains to be dealt with, for all the time since he fell from heaven in ch. 12, he has been behind the machinations of the Beast and the false prophet. Locusts had come out of the abyss in ch. 10 (BOTTOMLESS PIT, A.V.) when the star (angel) from heaven had opened it. It is here a place of temporary punishment (cf. the lake of fire); Satan now goes down a stage further still, to be restrained for 1,000 years. He is entirely subject to the purpose of God after the Messiah's decisive victory. This section with its curious story of the chaining of THE DRAGON, THAT OLD SERPENT WHICH IS THE DEVIL AND SATAN, has parallels with Persian and Egyptian folk-lore, with the book of Enoch and with Isa. 24. 21 f. On the significance of the millennium see the next section.

VI

THE MILLENNIAL CITY

(Ch. 20. 4-10; 21. 7 – 22. 2, 14, 15)

THE millennium, or the reign of Christ and the martyrs on earth for 1,000 years, is one of the strangest features of Revelation. It is full of symbolism and, of course, its details cannot be pressed. It is difficult to see, for instance, what there is left to be reigned over. But that is clearly a pointless question. We have to ask what John means by the symbolism and where he got it from. In one sense it is appropriate enough. Christ has conquered his enemies and reigns in triumph. Yet John seems to suggest that the victory is not complete and thus to contradict the N.T. emphasis, found particularly in the Epistle to the Hebrews, on the once-for-all aspect of Christ's work. For Satan is to be loosed again before the final judgment. What, we feel, does John *add* to his vision of the triumphant future by the millennium on earth? What is lacking in the new heaven and the new earth which this supplies? The question has continually puzzled interpreters, and the dominant tendency in the Church has been to equate the millennium with the life of the Church, and to regard the first resurrection as the death to sin and rising to righteousness characteristic of the life of the Christian community. But this was before apocalyptic literature was understood. We know now that there were two strains in Jewish thought of the future Messianic kingdom. One, going back to prophecy, looked to a glorious kingdom on earth. It is found, for instance, in Isa. 11, which has been alluded to several times in Revelation. In apocalyptic writing it developed immensely. Isa. 65. 20 ff. is an O.T. apocalyptic specimen, and it is developed in apocalyptic books like the Apocalypse of Baruch and parts of Enoch (1 Enoch). The other strain regarded the present world as hopeless, and looked to a temporary Messianic kingdom on a restored earth as a prelude to a new earth altogether. A good specimen of this can be found in our Apocrypha in 2 Esd. 7. 27 ff., where the Messiah reigns for 400 years and then dies. John incorporates both types of thought and, as usual, adapts them freely. Traditional details of the earthly kingdom, for instance, are used by him to describe the new Jerusalem in the new heaven and the new earth of ch. 21. f. And in fact very little is said of the millennium at all. John's reason for including it, apart from wishing to do justice to past prophecy, is to provide a distinctive reward for the martyrs.

We have repeatedly seen the reason for the stress on martyrdom in this book; John felt that a clear-cut issue of obedience or apostasy had arisen and would be intensified. Again his message has to be thought out afresh for each generation. It did lead at an early date to an unhealthy concentration on martyrdom, a foreshadowing of which can be seen in the letters of Ignatius written, only a decade or so after Revelation, as he was on his way to being martyred in Rome. Yet our day has seen situations arise as acute as those faced by the Christians for whom John wrote in Asia Minor in the last year of the reign of the Emperor Domitian.

As things stand John has in fact given symbolical expression to the thought that, whilst evil can never finally be overcome on this earth, yet right can achieve its temporary vindications over it. The relevance of the millennial city to us does not depend on our taking it as literal future history, and that relevance is discussed in greater detail on p. 133 ff. Nevertheless the doctrine of the millennium is peculiar in the N.T. to Revelation and cannot be regarded as having great authority, except in the sense of this paragraph (a sense which was probably of secondary importance in John's mind, for he was primarily concerned with rewarding the martyrs). The only other possible N.T. reference is the confusing passage in 1 Cor. 15. 24 ff. (on which see commentaries), but it is very doubtful.

20. 4-6: The First Resurrection

The THRONES of verse 4 come from that chapter which has so often been in John's mind, Dan. 7. 9, and the judgment from Dan. 7. 22, where it is given to 'the saints of the most High'. THEY is probably the martyrs, and calls to mind Matt. 19. 28 and Luke 22. 30. The rest of the verse summarises much of the past narrative of Revelation, especially ch. 13. The martyrs live again. How does John arrive at the number 1,000? It seems to be a combination of Gen. 2. 1 ff. and Ps. 90. 4. Another Enoch book, the Slavonic Enoch, makes the world last a week of seven days, each day being a thousand years, to be followed by an eighth day without time divisions, i.e. eternity. So John's vision may symbolise the perfectness of 1,000 years of Sabbaths after the seven days of the old creation and before the new creation of ch. 21 f. The fifth beatitude is found in verse 6, a blessing confined to the martyrs who are exempt from the final judgment and need have no fear of the second death (20. 14; 21. 8). The faithful who died peacefully, and the wicked, are in Hades awaiting the last judgment. The last part of verse 6 once more equates God and Christ. PRIESTS goes back to 1. 6 and 5. 10. John's treatment of the millennial city continues in 21. 7 – 22. 2, 14, 15. The text of the last three chapters of Revelation has become disarranged; on this see the note on p. 129, where a fuller discussion of the relevance of the millennial city will be found together with a commentary on the verses in ch. 21 and 22 which deal with it.

20. 7-10: Satan loosed and finally conquered

Again John uses the Gog-Magog visions of Ezek. 38 and 39 as in the previous chapter; in Ezekiel Gog is the name of a prince and Magog of his country; now they are symbolic of rulers and their peoples who obey the behests of Satan, whose function is deception, as before. John is here using the traditional Gog-Magog symbols to indicate God's final triumph over all that is opposed to his will, the consummation of what the victory of Christ has begun. THE BELOVED CITY of verse 9 appears to indicate that Jerusalem is the centre of the millennium, but it is a new Jerusalem on the site of the old apostate city. The FIRE is from Ezek. 38. 22. Satan now joins the Beast and the false prophet in the lake of fire to be TORMENTED DAY AND NIGHT FOR EVER AND EVER (see verse 14 below, and the note on 14. 10, p. 102).

(*Discussion of the Millennial City continued on p. 133*).

VII

THE LAST JUDGMENT

(Ch. 20. 11-15)

JOHN has at last reached his goal: the end of the world and the last judgment. We saw in the Introduction the necessity of expressing the beginning and end of the world in mythical language. John does not fail here to do justice to his theme and to prepare for the final vision of the new Jerusalem, now that the first heaven and the first earth have passed away. This they do in verse 11, leaving a GREAT WHITE THRONE as a centre of light in the midst of nothingness. Everything has vanished except God's authority. 'Heaven and earth shall pass away, but my words shall not pass away' (Matt. 24. 35, and see Isa. 24. 19 and 51. 6). The Father, who is reverentially not even named in the R.V., judges both SMALL AND GREAT (cf. John 5. 22); the Creator is the Judge. The judgment scene again has echoes of Dan. 7. 9 f. and 2 Esd. 6 and 7. The BOOKS contain the records of the deeds of men and the BOOK OF LIFE the names of the redeemed (see 3. 5 and note). According to one of the alternative readings of 13. 8 the names of the faithful have been in the book from the foundations of the world, for God had foreknowledge. Yet it is possible for a name to be removed (3. 5). John is inclined to see everything as fixed by divine plan, and yet he leaves scope for the undetermined consequences of human conduct. In this he is like Paul in Phil. 2. 12 ff. and his vision of judgment is like that of Paul in 2 Cor. 5. 10. All souls are given up for judgment, even from that unruly and troublesome element according to Hebrew thought and John's book —the sea, which GAVE UP THE DEAD, WHICH WERE IN IT (in the new earth there is no more sea, 21. 1). The dead are judged in verses 12 and 13 ACCORDING TO THEIR WORKS. This recalls 19. 8 where the 'fine linen is the righteous acts of the saints' and 14. 13 where it is said of the blessed dead who die in the Lord 'and their works do follow them'. In all these instances WORKS are the product of character; character results in RIGHTEOUS ACTS, and these are the necessary outward results of a character, a personality, which has been re-created by the work of Christ (cf. Matt. 7. 16; Gal. 5. 22 f.). Lastly, death and hell (R.V. Hades), having finished their task of keeping the dead awaiting judgment, are cast into THE LAKE OF FIRE which is THE SECOND DEATH, and the unrighteous who were NOT FOUND WRITTEN IN THE BOOK OF LIFE go with them. Death and Hades have been associated in 1. 18 and 6. 8: death as the fate of men, and Hades where they go after death. Although both righteous and unrighteous are involved, there is a sense in which death is an enemy (1 Cor. 15. 26, 54), for it stands in the way of the final immortality of the Christian and his full communion with Christ. So it is destroyed and banished from the ken of the righteous for ever.

The LAKE OF FIRE which elsewhere in the N.T. is called Gehenna, as can be gathered from the R.V. Margin of Mark 9. 43, Matt. 18. 9, etc., comes from the O.T. valley of Hinnom where (2 Kings 16. 3 and 21. 6) Ahaz and Manasseh caused their children to 'pass through fire' (i.e. child sacrifice was offered to Moloch; Jer. 7. 31 and Isa. 30. 33 refer to the place as Topheth). From these associations it came to stand for the burning fire of God's judgment, and hence the N.T. language about Gehenna (Hinnom). To John, just as the righteous from the book of life join Christ and the martyrs, so the wicked join Satan, the Beast and the false prophet, the Satanic trinity, in the lake of fire, the lowest depths of all. As the Introduction pointed out (p. 33), this seems to symbolise annihilation. John, of course, does not imagine that his descriptions are literal; fire is a good symbol for annihilation, for that is the function of fire. Also death is no more (according to 21. 4) in the new heaven and earth. We would interpret 20. 10 in this sense. Whether any soul will bring about its own destruction by refusing to respond to God's love to the very end, the N.T. on the whole gives us no sure means of deciding. John would seem to expect the majority to be in this category, to judge from his attitude in Revelation, but the plenitude of the Christian gospel is not wholly to be found in his book.

The re-arrangement of Chapters 20 – 22 and the Two Cities

From time to time it has been suggested in the course of this commentary (e.g. 14. 15-17) that John's work fell into the hands of an editor who rearranged his materials, sometimes inserting a note or two himself. When we come to the last chapters of Revelation, some such theory becomes almost essential. As they stand, the order of events in ch. 21 and 22 is most confusing; e.g. heaven and earth are passed away in 21. 1 and all evil forces have been eliminated by the end of chapter 20, yet in 21. 8 and 22. 14-15 we have a state of affairs where the wicked are still very much in existence. By far the simplest explanation is that the material in these chapters (indeed in chapter 20 also) has been disarranged, hence some attempt must be made to re-arrange it. That is why we have taken these two chapters together.

The first clue to the understanding of the right order of events in them is to realise that in all probability John meant to describe *two* cities. One of them, the first, is a sort of earthly paradise, a heavenly city set down in the midst of a pagan earth. To this city belong all the references to *contrasts* between those within and those without (e.g. 21. 8, 27). The other city is the Eternal City, the state of affairs which comes about when all evil has been overcome and God is all in all; it represents eternity, the state of everlasting bliss to which Christians look forward. It is referred to in such passages as 21. 1, 4; 22. 3. We may distinguish the two cities by calling the first the Millennial City, since it is the centre from which Christ and the martyred Church reign on the earth a thousand years (20. 4); the second we shall call the Eternal City. Perhaps the true sequence of events is now becoming clearer. It is probably as follows:

> The Millennial City descends from heaven, and Christ and his saints rule in it on the earth a thousand years: 20. 4-10.
> Description of the Millennial City: 21. 7 – 22. 2 and 22. 14-15.
> The Last Judgment: 20. 11-15.
> The New Heaven and Earth; the Eternal City: 21. 1-6 and 22. 3-5.
> Epilogue 22. 6-13 and 16-21.

It is always confusing when verses and chapters have to be re-arranged like this; but the main scheme to bear in mind is:

> 20. 4-10; 21. 7 – 22. 2; 22. 14, 15: The Millennial City.
> 20. 11-15: The Last Judgment.
> 21. 1-6; 22. 3-5: The Eternal City.

We have still to ask: what does John mean by these two cities? As so often happens, in order to answer this adequately we have to examine John's sources and materials. The notion of 'the city of the gods', of some celestial city far above the earth, is a very old one. It may have originated in Babylonian mythology. Certainly the Babylonians had the idea; as we have seen, they believed that the stars were gods, or the abode of the gods. Being among the earliest scientific astronomers, they observed the procession of the Zodiac, named the various constellations in it, and regarded it as *par excellence* the dwelling place of the gods. The Greeks in their turn made use of the idea, and we may probably trace in Plato's theory of the ideal world the original influence of Babylonian astronomical mythology. But the Greeks had their own intellectual genius, and in Plato's philosophy the crude, localised 'city of the gods' of the Babylonians has been refined into the world of intellectual reality, beyond time and space, the realm of mind and reason, the unchanging, eternal world of thought. In the meantime the genius of the Hebrews had been at work on this notion also, and they too made their own peculiar use of it. There were two things that the Hebrews were concerned about above everything in the universe: the moral government of the world, and the living God. How could the two be reconciled? Between 700 B.C. and 200 B.C. the little country of Palestine was invaded by one aggressor nation after another: Assyria, Babylon, Persia, Greece. How could the living God allow the wicked to prosper thus? How was his chosen people to be vindicated? The answer which most Hebrew thinkers had found by Jesus' time lay in their notion of 'The Kingdom of God'. This paradisal country, this 'city of the gods', which the Babylonians believed to be permanently located among the stars and which the Greeks had dissolved into a purely intellectual reality, was to be brought down to earth by the living God. Then at last wickedness would be punished and righteousness vindicated. But even within this future kingdom some minds among the Jews could see the need for a distinction: the Kingdom when it came would have to effect two purposes. The earth would have to be purged, and everything would have to be made secure for the future, for the eternal future. Hence some writers declared that there would be two Kingdoms: a perfect Kingdom on earth, which would last a limited time, and a final and eternal Kingdom beyond time and space, which would wind up history altogether and leave all God's purposes finally fulfilled.

This Jewish treatment of 'the city of the gods' John has taken over. And, when we look at it in the light of Christianity, we can see how appropriate for his purpose was the contemporary Jewish notion of two kingdoms, a temporal and an eternal. John was a Christian and believed therefore that in some sense God's Kingdom had come. Jesus Christ had brought down to earth from heaven the eternal Kingdom of God. In him men and women could, here and now, under the conditions of time and space, enjoy the blessedness of communion with God. But at the same time there lay before every Christian the hope of an infinitely deeper experience of this communion after death. Eternal life, as the Fourth Gospel teaches, begins here and now for the Christian, but it will not always be eternal life under the conditions of space and time. It is the same eternal life under all conditions, but no well-informed Christian imagined that he was supposed to ignore the distinction between life in the flesh and life beyond the grave. Hence in John's description of the Millennial City we may see his picture of the Church Militant as she should be and as, in God's eyes, she is called to be. It is an inspiring, and even awesome, vision of what the Church is called to be *on earth*; hence the contrast between those within and those without. In the Eternal City we have, not a picture (for this is impossible), but an intuition, a symbol, of the condition of the Church Triumphant, the Church as she will be when time and space are no more, as she *is* now in heaven, because eternity is, as St. Augustine reminds us, everywhere always.

It is interesting to notice here that John is apparently conscious of the pagan origin of the symbols he uses, since he goes out of his way to repudiate what is pagan in them. In 21. 19-20 we find what must seem to some of us an unnecessarily detailed description of the precious stones with which the foundations of the Millennial City were decorated. R. H. Charles points out that each of these precious stones represents a sign of the Zodiac (the identification was conventional in contemporary astronomy), but John has given his list of precious stones in the reverse order to that in which the sun passes through the signs of the Zodiac. This order is deliberately adopted by John and is intended as a repudiation of the pagan associations of the Zodiac. Roughly the same precious stones are described as forming the ornamentation of the High Priest's breastplate in Ex. 28. 17-20, so John may have felt that he was justified in bringing them into his description, as long as he made it clear that he did not intend any pagan associations.

At this point it would seem best to consider an objection that may well have occurred to the reader. What evidence is there that John really meant by his Two Cities what we have said he meant? Why interpret them as an ideal picture of the Church Militant and an actual picture of the Church in eternity? Is it not more likely that John intended at least his Millennial City to be taken literally? What right have we to explain its literalness away in this convenient fashion? Now it is quite true that John did mean at least the fact of his Millennial City to be taken literally (some at least of the details he could not possibly have expected to be taken in this way—see the note on 21. 16); as we have seen on p. 124, his main interest in the Millennial City arose from his desire that the martyrs should be rewarded. But when we have said that, we have not yet explained the significance of the Two Cities, either for the Christians of John's day, or for us. Why give this description of these cities if they were *merely* future events? John is nothing if not concerned with action; all through his book runs the note of urgency, the call to action. The last thing we would expect him to do would be to describe, in great and often highly symbolic detail, a state of affairs which was to be merely a future event. We cannot read ch. 21 and 22 without asking: what does it mean here and now? And of course, when we do so, we find that John is saying something which concerns all Christians of all ages. Largely through our knowledge of the O.T., and of the way in which the authors of the N.T. interpreted it, we can understand in terms of our own day most of what John is saying. Implied in John's description of this city of the martyrs is the belief that this ideal state of affairs *was possible*, that all these qualities and virtues belonging to the ideal church were relevant. Indeed it is this conviction that has inspired all Christian efforts for the betterment of mankind. If it were not so, these chapters are more akin to the guide book than the profound interpretation of the will of God in human history which we have found throughout the previous chapters of Revelation.

The Millennial City (continued from 20. 6)

We may therefore proceed with a clear conscience to examine the details of the Millennial City, applying them to the vocation of the Church in all ages. The first thing that strikes us is the contrast between those who are members of the Church and those who are not which we meet in 21. 8 and 27, and 22. 14-15. It is this which is perhaps the basis of all the other qualities of the Church on earth described by John. Needless to say, it is a note we encounter throughout the N.T. (cf. John 17. 14; Phil. 2. 15).

The phrase MAKETH A LIE in 21. 27 implies an attitude of fundamental insincerity; it is the opposite of the emphasis on 'doing the truth' in 1 John 1. 6.

We have already (19. 9) met the striking image of the Bride and Bridegroom for the relation of his Church to Christ. Here (21. 9—and in 21. 2, where it refers to the Eternal City) John repeats it. It has a long genealogy; in the fertility religion which the Jews encountered when they entered Palestine, the conception of God as being married to the land, and hence in some sense to the people of the land, was central. No doubt those primitive Hebrews accepted it as they accepted most other elements in the Canaanite religion. But gradually we see the deepest thinkers in Israel refining and spiritualising the idea and making it the vehicle for expressing the most intimate and personal contact between God and man. First Hosea (Hos. 2), then Ezekiel (Ezek. 16), then an anonymous prophet of perhaps the fifth century B.C. (Isa. 61. 10) carried on this process, till it was ready to be taken up and given a Messianic interpretation by Jesus himself (Mark 2. 19). John has matched the courage of the Hebrew prophets in turning to their own use a mode of thinking so much associated with paganism, by appropriating to the relation of Christ to his Church a figure used by them to express the relation of God to Israel.

Next in 21. 10 and 12 we have two details which are rather absurd if taken literally, but highly significant if regarded as symbolic. The City descends out of heaven. This is not a heavenly transformation scene, but an iteration of something which we meet all through the N.T.: the Church is not something which we build, it is something given us by God. It all stems from the fundamental Christian affirmation that we do not save ourselves: we have already been redeemed by Christ. Our task is not to conquer the Promised Land, but to enter on the inheritance prepared for us by God. If those who speak glibly of our 'building the Kingdom of God' would meditate a little on this verse, they might see cause for altering their terminology. The other detail is the immense height of the walls round the City; its meaning is just the same as 21. 8, etc., Christians are a people apart. But an interesting point here is that if we take verses 16 and 17 literally, we must imagine a city with walls 1,500 miles high and only 216 feet thick! It should surely make us pause before we assert that John is telling a plain tale here that should be taken *au pied de la lettre*. With these measurements compare the number of the citizens of the heavenly city in 7. 4.

The wall has TWELVE FOUNDATIONS (verse 14) on which are written the names of the twelve Apostles of the Lamb. Once more John has changed his metaphor and woven one more figure expressing the relation of Christ to his Church into the wonderful tapestry of his symbolism. Christ is the building (John 2. 19; 1 Cor. 6. 19; Col. 2. 7) or else he is the chief corner-stone (Eph. 2. 20). The Apostles are called the foundations because it is on the faith which they proclaimed that the Church is founded and by which alone she stands. Compare the collect for St. Simon and St. Jude's Day in the Anglican *Book of Common Prayer*, which begins 'O Almighty God, who hast built thy Church upon the foundation of the Apostles and Prophets, Jesus Christ himself being the head corner-stone . . .'. Perhaps in verse 16 we can detect an echo of pagan ethics; the architectural detail is taken from Ezek. 43, but the 'foursquare man without flaw', as one old Greek poet expresses it, was admired in antiquity. The Holy of Holies in Solomon's temple was also a perfect cube: 1 Kings 6. 20. The precious stones in verse 19 f. can show a venerable lineage also. One version of the Paradise story says that they were found in the garden of Eden (Ezek. 28. 13), and the anonymous prophet of the Exile foresees a renewed Jerusalem adorned with precious stones (Isa. 54. 11). We can hardly imagine that a man of John's insight put these in just for the pretty effect, and we may conclude that in Paradise Regained the jewels would appear as the virtues and graces of the fully sanctified.

We have emphasised the difference between the Millennial City and the Eternal City, but in verse 22 we realise that they have one thing in common—unbroken communion with the living God. The condition of the blessed in eternity is to be a fuller measure of, not a different experience from, their highest point of fellowship with God on earth. Indeed, all we really know for sure about the state of those who have fallen asleep in Christ is that they are indeed in Christ; we should not ask to know more. Notice in 21. 23 that the Lamb is the light of the Millennial City together with the glory of God (cf. John 8. 12) whereas in 22. 5 the Lord God alone gives light to the Eternal City. Jesus was more especially perhaps connected with the city of martyrs. In verse 24 we have one of the few references in the N.T. to the relation of the Church to the nations; THE NATIONS OF THEM WHICH ARE SAVED (R.V. has 'the nations' only). This may merely mean 'the multitudes of them that are saved', but it is certainly not a strained interpretation to suggest that the cultural values and varieties which are enshrined in what is meant by 'nationality' at its best are approved by God and can be used to his glory in the world-wide Church. Differentiation of culture and race rather than an independent status of self-government is what 'nation' suggested in the world of John's day. It would be an anachronism to read into it the idea of a sovereign nation-state with which nationalism in the modern world has familiarised us. In 22. 2 there is a suggestion, but only a suggestion, that Christianity has an application in the international sphere. How, we are not told.

The last detail of the Millennial City concerns the tree of life (cf. 2. 7). We first meet the tree of life in Gen. 3. 22; Adam and Eve are banished from Eden lest they should eat its fruit. It represents immortality, eternal life. Now at last, almost at the end of the great drama of the Bible, man may return and legitimately enjoy the blessing which he was banished for illegitimately desiring. And this blessing has not been achieved by man himself as the result of his own efforts. It has descended OUT OF HEAVEN FROM GOD in the holy Jerusalem. God has himself in Jesus Christ taken the initiative, and restored to us the eternal life for which he intended us when he created us.

VIII

THE ETERNAL CITY

(Ch. 21. 1-6; 22. 3-5)

We have seen that in his picture of the Eternal, as distinguished from the Millennial, City John is telling us something of the Church in eternity as distinguished from the Church still militant on earth. In a sense therefore this is an imagination of what is to happen in the future, and yet, when we are concerned with eternity, to speak of 'the future' is rather absurd. We are dealing with the relations of time and eternity. Eternity is not just 'a long time', but a condition outside time altogether. We can only imagine it in terms of future time, but here, if anywhere, we must bear in mind that we are dealing with symbols. So we may say that the Church in eternity is in one sense the Church as she is now in God's eyes, as she is in deepest truth; at any rate that she will not be really and fully the Church until what is said of the Eternal City is entirely true of her. The Lamb, remember, was 'slain from the foundation of the world' according to one reading of 13. 8.

We turn, then, to examine the details of the Eternal City, contained in 21. 1-6 and 22. 3-5. One of the first features of the Eternal City appears perhaps a little strange: THERE WAS NO MORE SEA (21. 1). It is true that the Hebrews were never a seafaring people, and we can detect a horror and wonder at the sea sometimes in the O.T.; but the reason for this detail goes deeper than that. The sea in Babylonian mythology represented the element of chaos which God had to overcome before he created the earth; Tiamat, the primeval chaos monster, was connected with the sea, and God's triumph over Tiamat could be represented as a triumph over the sea (cf. Ps. 74. 13-14; Isa. 51. 10). So 'there was no more sea' means that the element of disorder in the universe is done away. Then in 21. 3 John tells us of another great feature of the Eternal City: THE TABERNACLE OF GOD IS WITH MEN. The use of the word tabernacle brings us back to the O.T., where the sojourn of Israel in the wilderness is narrated. There the sacred tent in which God was believed to dwell was called the tabernacle. In later times the Hebrew word for the tabernacling of God, the *Shekinah*, was used as a reverential way of referring to God, as we speak of 'the presence' today. The author of the Fourth Gospel takes up this idea and Christianises it. In the magnificent prologue to his gospel (John 1. 1-14) he wishes to describe the incarnation of the Word of God, Jesus Christ, and he uses this concept of the 'presence' or 'tabernacling' of God: 'and the word was made flesh and dwelt among us'. The R.V. margin reads 'tabernacled', a much better translation. It is likely that the author of the Fourth Gospel deliberately chose the Greek word *ĕskenōsen* because it recalled in sound the Hebrew *shekinah*; he wanted to assert that the very presence of God had come down among men. John uses the same word here for 'will dwell', and a noun from the same root for 'tabernacle'. Now, in eternity, that which the Incarnation secured in principle has come to pass in full reality: man is fully and for ever united and reconciled to God. With HE WILL DWELL WITH THEM cf. Isa. 7. 14 (Immanuel=God with us) quoted in Matt. 1. 23.

In verses 5 and 6 of ch. 21 we meet a series of phrases and ideas which have already occurred, either in Revelation itself or in the N.T. generally. Thus I MAKE ALL THINGS NEW not only echoes the NEW HEAVEN AND THE NEW EARTH of 21. 1, but also recalls the 'new creation' of Paul's thought (cf. 2 Cor. 5. 17). That word 'new' is the keynote of the N.T.: the new Israel, the new Covenant, the new commandment, the new wine of Jesus' teaching. Then all the phrases in verse 6 have occurred before in Revelation itself, and of course the notion of THE WATER OF LIFE belongs also to the Fourth Gospel (e.g. John 4. 10). The phrase IT IS DONE announced the destruction of Babylon in 16. 17. The significance of all this well-used Christian language recurring here is not just that it gives solemn emphasis coming like this at the end of the book; but that all these blessings, which are given us in part and in principle and under the limitations of time and space and sin and partial error in the Church on earth, through the life, death, and resurrection of Christ, are to be ours in full and without any of these limitations and qualifications when we enter the condition of eternity. John is simply giving content and fuller meaning to Paul's vision of the time when God shall be all in all (1 Cor. 15. 28).

In 22. 3 John tells us THERE SHALL BE NO MORE CURSE. This completes the statement of 21. 1: THERE WAS NO MORE SEA. As that referred to the element of disorder in nature, so this refers to the element of disorder in the moral sphere. From the most ancient times the notion had prevailed that conduct which broke God's laws brought a curse on the doer. This hereditary curse is the theme of the greatest of the ancient Greek tragedies which survive, the *Oresteia* of Aeschylus. So also we hear of the primal curse at the fall of man in Gen. 3. 17, and all through the O.T. cursings are promised to those who disobey (e.g. Deut. 27. 15 ff.). St. Paul (Gal. 3. 13) goes so far as to say that Christ 'redeemed us from the curse of the law, being made a curse on our behalf'; that is to say that he, taking the consequences of sin on himself, enables us to overcome the sin which prevents our communion with God. Now at last in eternity there is to be no more sin at all. It is no longer a question of Christ affording us the means to overcome sin; sin has been finally overcome. This contrasts of course, strikingly with the Millennial City, where 'without are dogs and sorcerers', etc. (22. 15). HIS SERVANTS SHALL SERVE HIM in 22. 3 may sound rather like tautology to us, but remember that it is eternity which John is describing, and it would be by no means obvious that 'service' is necessarily to be our lot in eternity if John had not mentioned it. We moderns, however, should beware of interpreting service in its modern sense of bustling action. John may well mean by 'serve', worship (the Greek word not much later came to mean worship). The great point John wanted to make was that we are still to be able to devote the *will* to God in eternity, and worship is primarily a matter of the will. He had in mind no doubt the Platonic idea of eternity, which promises us the condition of being

'a pulse in the eternal Mind, no less',

and he wanted to distinguish the Christian doctrine of eternity from this (cf. Rom. 12. 1, where R.V. Margin translates the same word as 'worship').

The description of the Eternal City ends very appropriately in 22. 4 and 5 with a reminder of that personal communion with God which is the goal and essence of true life and true happiness and is perfectly consummated in eternity, THEY SHALL SEE HIS FACE. This privilege was denied to Moses (Ex. 33. 20). The more we meditate on the meaning of those five words, the more profound and inconceivable what they attempt to express becomes to us. We may well have been perplexed and annoyed at the broken and fragmentary nature of the descriptions of the Two Cities which we must try to extract from these last two chapters. But their very difficulty will be not without value if it reminds us of the fragmentary nature of our knowledge of true reality now, and of how impossible it is adequately to describe the glory of what is beyond space and time; 'For now we see through a glass, darkly; but then face to face' (1 Cor. 13. 12).

The Transformation of the Old Testament Background in Chapters 20-22

We have already noticed (Introduction, p. 36) that much of these last two chapters is founded on the O.T., and especially on the later chapters of Isaiah. It is worth while observing, however, the great beauty of John's treatment of these O.T. prophecies, a most fitting end to a book which is so full of O.T. echoes. The various authors of these later chapters of Isaiah[1] all look forward to a time when Israel will be restored, indeed restored in an ideal manner, almost a golden age for the Jews. But at their best these hopes are material and temporal. John takes these hopes and promises and gives them a far deeper spiritual and eternal content. For example in Rev. 21. 19 the precious stones come from Isa. 54. 11 and 12. The most that the prophet of Israel's exile in Babylon could have meant by that passage was that his people would once more live in peace and prosperity amid beautiful surroundings in Judaea. John makes it refer to the everlasting beauty of the truly Christian character nurtured in the faith and life of the Church. Similarly in Rev. 22. 12 God is represented as saying 'Behold, I come quickly; and my reward is with me', an echo of Isa. 40. 10 and 62. 11. The most that the reward can mean in the O.T. passages is the restoration of the Jews to Palestine or their deliverance from some temporal oppressor. In Revelation the reward is nothing less than full and eternal communion with God for those who will accept it. Finally, it may be that in 21. 16 we have an echo, not of Isaiah, but of Genesis. We have seen the astonishing height of the walls; they represent the absolute distinction between Christian and non-Christian. But they may also mean that now at last God has himself built the 'city and the tower whose top may reach unto heaven' of Gen. 11. 4. The Tower of Babel is in origin a confused memory of those *ziggurats* or sacred towers which the Babylonians used to build, thinking thus to construct a kind of artificial link between earth and heaven. John, as so often in his book, baptises the pagan conception. The true link between heaven and earth is now built by God in Jesus Christ.

[1] John, no doubt, believed that they all came from the pen of the historical Isaiah, the son of Amoz. But it seems to make no difference to his interpretation.

IX

EPILOGUE

(Ch. 22. 6-13, 16-21)

All we have to do now is to examine the verses in these last chapters which do not refer to either of the Two Cities. They amount to some thirteen in all and form John's conclusion to his book. They are all found in 22. 6-13 (14 and 15 belong, as we have seen, to the Millennial City) and 16-21. There is some doubt about verses 18 and 19. It has been suggested that these two verses were not written by John, but by the editor who assembled ch. 21 and 22. They seem sufficiently *gauche* in themselves; there is slight linguistic evidence against them; and it does not seem very likely that John expected a sufficiently lengthy period to elapse after the writing of his book for there to be any fear of interpolations creeping in. On the other hand, interpolations in contemporary apocalypses were so common that John may have wished to guard against them.

With 22. 8 compare 19. 10. There is some evidence that the Jews of John's time did practise the worship of angels. It was a consequence of their greatly increased sense of the awefulness and power, and therefore remoteness, of God. Heretical sects which had already formed within and outside the Church in John's day also tended to emphasise the distance between God and man, and to fill up the gap by means of a hierarchy of angelic and superhuman mediators.

It is likely that John had people of this sort in mind when he related these two incidents. In verse 10 John is forbidden to seal the book; contrast Jewish apocalypses, which were all sealed.

Verse 11 is the last reference to the divine wrath with which we have been so much concerned in this commentary. It is a very appropriate one to end on, since it gives us the principle according to which the divine wrath acts. Each man must accept the consequences of his own character and actions: hell, wrath, and damnation are nothing but the working out to their final conclusions of what each one of us does to our own selves as long as we refuse the love of God. In the same way, obedience to God results in our discovering still greater areas of obedience: 'Unto him that hath shall be given.'

The epithets of Jesus in verse 16 bring us back to the first three chapters with their ever varied refrain of epithets; see 2. 28. THE ROOT AND THE OFFSPRING OF DAVID emphasises the true Messiahship of Jesus. The actual genealogy from David can hardly mean very much to the non-Jewish Church in any age. But Jesus' claim to kingship is of the utmost significance. It is interesting that the author of the Fourth Gospel (who probably wrote at much the same time as our John) emphasises far more the kingship than the Messiahship of Christ in his passion-narrative. We have already seen that John knew of the old pagan belief in the stars as gods (note on 9. 1). In calling Jesus THE BRIGHT AND MORNING STAR we have a last example of John's claiming 'the heathen for his inheritance'. In Isa. 14. 12 (a later passage not by the historical Isaiah) Babylon is compared to a fallen star, a great heavenly being who has been overthrown; and in Job 38. 7 all 'the morning stars' means all God's ministering angels. Here in most beautiful language John claims for Christ a place 'better than the angels'. (Heb. 1. 4). In verse 17 Christ himself and his bride, the community which he had purchased (19. 7), say COME.

SURELY I COME QUICKLY. AMEN. EVEN SO, COME, LORD JESUS. Cf. 1 Cor. 16. 22, where the punctuation should be 'let him be anathema. Maran Atha.' *Maran Atha* is Aramaic for 'our Lord cometh'. Thus with a dramatic reference to the coming of the Lord ends the last book in the Bible. The very fact that it ends on a note so much at variance with the prevailing outlook of Western civilisation should make us think. Even more significant is the fact that this note is one which occurs constantly throughout the N.T. Christianity is not a faith which bids us look for a gradual upward march of man till he reaches an ideal state of civilisation. Rather it bids us believe in an active, living God, whose love and whose wrath are alike revealed in the events of human history, a God who has played the decisive part in that history when he sent Jesus Christ among us, and in whose ultimate control of events lies our sole confidence. Only if we hold this faith can we retain any real hope in this present world, and answer courageously with John: 'Come, Lord Jesus.' It is the only faith that can dare to hold its own in the atomic era.